# Nourishing Wisdom

# Nourishing Wisdom

## A New Understanding of Eating

MARC DAVID

Bell Tower/New York

Published by Bell Tower, an imprint of Harmony Books, a division of Crown Publishers, Inc., 201 East 50th Street, New York, New York 10022. Member of the Crown Publishing Group.

HARMONY and colophon and BELL TOWER and colophon are trademarks of Crown Publishers, Inc.

Manufactured in the United States of America

Library of Congress Cataloging-in-Publication Data
David, Marc.
    Nourishing wisdom : a new understanding of eating / Marc David.
        p.   cm.
    1. Food habits—Psychological aspects.   2. Nutrition—
Psychological aspects.   I. Title.
    TX357.D32   1991
    613.2—dc20                                                          90-46675
                                                                              CIP

ISBN 0-517-57636-8
10 9 8 7 6 5 4 3 2 1
First Edition

For my mother, Rachel, a wise, loving, and nourishing being, and for my father, Sidney, the rock in my life that never failed.

# Contents

# Acknowledgments

It is a beautiful gift for me to honor publicly those who have taught me, supported me, and stood by my side. My uncle Ronald Cohen lit the creative spark in me long ago and has nurtured its growth ever since. My sister, Rhonda, has been loving, dedicated, and firm in her belief in me. My dear friend Rajiv has taught me what it means to be a friend and a true brother.

My wife, Gabriella, has been teacher, editor, cook, companion, lover, healer, resident goddess, and a long list of other things. In short, magic.

Other friends and relatives have given deeply of themselves: Sandra Cohen, Alvaro Ortiz, Lori Davis, Miriah Stuart, Sarah Novick, Jessica Franke, Joan Berry, Wellington Lee, and Dave Lewis.

I am indebted to my teachers: Yogi Amrit Desai, a wise sage, masterful player, and compassionate guide—his teachings on the art of living help form the glue for my work; Michael Hughes, teacher, brother, healer, and musician of the soul—I thank him for introducing me to my body. Robert Greenway, the late Gordon Tappan, and Morris Berman (who's famous but nobody knows it) have also seeded my thoughts with their timeless wisdom.

Mitchell Ditkoff was the midwife for this book at its earliest stage, providing expert editing, consulting, and loving friendship. Jeffrey and Rusty Cohen were great basketball buddies when I needed them most. Special thanks to my agent, Sarah Jane Freymann, for her friendship, professionalism, and belief in my work. My editor at Bell Tower, Toinette Lippe, has been a trusted reader, wise woman, loving friend, and a writer's dream.

Final thank-you's to Gudni Gunarsson for our special conversations, Navin for our cutting edge talks about food and nutrition, Bharat (Tom Jackman)—best buddy and trusted copilot—and to my wonderful friends at the Kripalu Yoga Center.

# Introduction

For millions of people food and diet are very problematic. Instead of being a source of nourishment, food has become an area of conflict and confusion—endless weight-loss dramas, eating disorders, cravings, addictions, body image obsessions, and never-ending searches for "the best" nutritional system. Even if you have never suffered from any of these complaints, you probably feel overwhelmed by all the books, articles, and "experts"—each with something different to say—and would welcome some clear and useful guidance about eating.

Read a book on scientific nutrition, and eating appears to be simply a biological process: nutrient intake, digestion, and cellular assimilation. Read a book about dieting, and eating is presented as a war. It is you against the calories, you against your body fat, and you against your desires. Read any number of books on "natural" ways of nutrition, and eating may be presented as a divinely ordained system. Disregard its commandments, and wrathful gods will punish you with ill health. Read any popular cookbook or food magazine, and eating is presented solely as an affair of the palate where each recipe is orchestrated for your sensuous pleasure. Read any book on eating disorders, and you will realize that our attitude to food may be literally a matter of life and death.

The question then arises, Is there a way to explain the diversity of perspectives on nutrition and the different ways of relating to food? Is there one "true" way to eat? Are there common dietary principles that all eaters share, regardless of their orientation? And, more to the point, can we make sense of the conflicting impulses that exist side by side in our mind—the desire to eat "healthy" foods versus the desire to eat forbidden ones, the desire to overeat versus the desire to lose weight, the desire to help ourselves versus the unconscious desire to self-destruct.

Many of us are searching for a sensible source of information about diet that explains the complexities of the eater's mind. We want a way to understand our relationship to food and body without being told that what we are eating is "wrong" or being harassed into following another "breakthrough" diet system. Virtually all diet and nutrition books promote a specific way to eat, a new diet gimmick, or the illusory promise of permanent weight loss, eternal health, and boundless energy. Few books nourish us at deeper levels.

Eating is a vastly unexplored area in psychology. Only recently have researchers begun to question what happens in the mind when it sets itself the task of feeding the body. *Nourishing Wisdom* elucidates the psychology of eating by mapping out the fundamental principles of the eater's mind. It provides a framework to understand the different perspectives on eating. It details the essential ingredients of a successful working relationship to diet. Most important, it offers practical tools that can help you transform your relationship to food.

Many people talk more openly about their sex life than about their eating habits. As public a phenomenon as eating is, our personal issues with food and body image may be the best-kept secrets we have. If the estimates of forty to sixty-five million dieters in America is anywhere near correct, that amounts to a great deal of dissatisfaction. Wherever we stand as individuals, the facts show that collectively our relationship to food harbors a deep source of self-rejection and pain.

Many of us look to food to give us something it cannot provide. We want satisfaction, but we work toward it in very dissatisfied ways. Often, in our attempts to rid ourselves of negative food habits, we adopt strategies that make the *conflict* about having the habit more damaging than the habit itself.

We criticize ourselves because we cannot live up to our impossibly high standards or because we do not understand how to do the simple things that we know would transform us. How many times have I heard someone say, "I know what my problem is. I know what I need to do for myself. I just don't do it!"

For those of us who have said this, perhaps it would be instructive to know that human beings need to *learn* about eating. We need to learn how to sustain our bodies properly, manage our energy, cultivate positive habits, and allow food to nourish rather than punish us.

Unlike animals who *feed,* human beings *eat.* That is, food for us is largely cultural and psychological rather than instinctual. What is especially intriguing is that not only do human beings learn about eating, but everybody seems to learn something different. Every eater has a theory about what eating is and what should be eaten. Seldom will you see two dogs arguing about the best diet for the canine kingdom, or a group of elephants going on a weight-loss program to feel better about themselves. Animals require neither diet books nor nutritionists.

By learning about the body, we human beings are able to alter our own biology. We have the capacity to transform the body with the mind. And yet we often use this ability of the mind to disable the body and create needless emotional turmoil with food. For we operate on an extensive system of erroneous beliefs and false hopes when it comes to losing weight, perfecting our diet, or just plain eating. These concepts give rise to an assortment of behavior patterns that prevent us from experiencing the natural joy of eating.

*Nourishing Wisdom* places nutrition in the larger contexts of spiritual and psychological development. It focuses on living and thinking correctly as the vehicle for eating correctly. It maneuvers us out of the maze of nutritional "shoulds" and "shouldn'ts" and into a realm where the body is met on its own terms. Each of us has our own life-style, set of beliefs, and range of biochemical requirements. *Nourishing Wisdom* helps us discover the dynamic and changing nature of the body and reveals how our relationship to food can teach us about our relationship to life.

# Nourishing Wisdom

# 1

# The Missing Ingredient

An old Jewish folktale tells of a father and small son who built a lifelike dummy to scare the birds from their garden. The birds ignored the dummy and continued to eat the crops. Disappointed, the father surrendered the garden to the birds, but the boy kept hope. He visited an old rabbi on his deathbed and told him of their plight. The rabbi said, "Here, take this," and wrote something on a small scrap of paper. "On this paper is written the name of God. Place it in the dummy's mouth and your garden will be saved."

The boy dashed to the garden and placed the piece of paper in the dummy's mouth. Instantly the dummy came to life. The birds scattered and the dummy jumped off its pole and began tending the garden with the skills of an expert farmer. The townspeople soon discovered the miraculous dummy could also build houses, plow fields, and even sing and dance. When approached with questions about the nature of life, the dummy spoke with great wisdom, softening the hardest hearts in the village.

But, alas, the townspeople grew lazy and wanted him to work rather than teach. They pulled at his arms and legs, saying, "Come, plow my fields"; "No, come fix my house"; "No, come mend our clothes." In the scuffle the piece of paper with the name of God fell from the dummy's mouth, and immediately he collapsed in a lifeless heap.

The most skilled craftsmen were summoned, but none could bring the dummy back to life. Then one of the villagers exclaimed, "Something is missing, some vital piece of the dummy must have fallen off as we wrestled with it." The villagers searched, but all they could find was a scrap of paper with some gibberish on it, and they threw it back on the ground. Sadly, the little boy picked up the piece of paper, placed it in his pocket, and as he walked to the garden he heard the distant voices of the townspeople saying, "Something is missing . . . something is missing. . . ."

In my search for a coherent approach to nutrition amid all the conflicting theories, I realized that the missing ingredient in most dietary systems was a spiritual context, a way to see the sacredness and interconnectedness of all things. We are more than just a body, a tongue, and an assortment of nutritional requirements. We are a soul clothed in the elements of the earth, journeying in a realm where matter and spirit unite in human form. The body serves as a sacred vessel fashioned through millions of years of evolution to carry the spark of life, "the name of God," as it were. Without that little piece of paper in our mouth, we are nothing more than a "dummy," a lifeless collection of elements.

Food is not merely something we eat. It is a ceaseless reminder that we are mortal, earthbound, hungry, and in need. We are bound by a biological imperative that forever keeps us returning to the soil, plants, animals, and running waters for replenishment. Eating is life. Each time we eat, the soul continues its earthly journey. With every morsel of food swallowed a voice within says, "I choose life. I choose to eat, for I yearn for something more."

But what is this something more?

The great twentieth-century thinker Aldous Huxley refers to a view of humanity called "the perennial philosophy," which represents the collective wisdom of all the great spiritual traditions. According to the perennial philosophy we are more than a body and more than a mind. We are of a spiritual source. From it we emerge at birth, and to it we return at death. And whenever the spiritual source seems a faint memory, we yearn for its presence. Some call this yearning "religion" or "faith," others call it "the quest for happiness" or "inner peace."

It is here in the spiritual realm that our journey into the mind of the eater begins. For beneath our nutritional theories, eating habits, and food obsessions, beneath our insecurities and embarrassment about the body, beneath any doubt as to the basic goodness of existence, there dwells within us a condition of wholeness born from the spiritual source. This is not a state of pristine perfection and eternal comfort where all problems disappear and we wallow in meditative mush. It is a condition of timeless identification with the Divine, where life and death, pleasure and pain, success and failure, happiness and discontent, are met with equal acceptance. It is a state of equanimity where we feel fully human, completely alive, and in love with life no matter what happens.

According to the perennial philosophy, human beings are separated from the spiritual source for one reason alone: We believe we are separate. Each of us holds the false belief that "I am separate from all creation, I am alone, and I am not enough as I am." Consequently, the state of wholeness exists only as a potential within us. And though it lies buried like a dormant seed, all beings instinctively intuit its existence. Our purpose in life is to rejoin the spiritual source and embody it here and now. This is the "something more" we continually seek.

With this perspective, nutrition can now be seen in a new light. Placed within a spiritual context, the ultimate goal of any dietary philosophy is to take us fully *into* the body, and *beyond* the body. That is, by taking us fully into the body our dietary system must enable us to experience the maximum physical benefits of food—good health, the delight of eating, and the fulfillment of nutrient needs. By taking us fully beyond the body, our dietary philosophy must serve to remind us that we are feeding more than just a body. Nutrition not only keeps the body healthy and attractive, it maintains it as a vehicle in the service of the Divine. By nourishing the body with joy and reverence, we nourish the spark of life within the body. And when the body yields to disease and decay (which no amount of vegetables or vitamins can prevent), we are left with the knowledge that good nutrition is important but can take us only so far. The deeper nourishment that sustains heart and soul is what ultimately matters most.

In many ancient traditions the body is considered sacred, and great care is taken to ensure its health and longevity. Yogis, for example, developed an extensive system of practices unequaled in thoroughness. These center on maintaining and developing the body through diet, exercise, postures, medicines, methods of breathing, and a host of life-style practices. The Taoists, too, developed unique methods combining martial arts, visualizations, sound, subtle energy cultivation, and healing food. Despite such strong emphasis on health and longevity, these traditions view the body not as God, but as a vehicle *for* God.

In the West the body is often worshipped as if its perfection and health were the highest goal we could attain. Few people escape the media images and cultural bias toward ideal bodies and perfect health. More than anything else we want to believe that the physical form will last forever. As Krishna says in the *Bhagavad Gita*, "Of all the wonders in the world, the greatest wonder is this: That no man, though he sees others die all around him, believes he himself will perish."

Indeed, living in a body with all the considerations of pain, disease, and death causes us to confront our greatest fears about the nature of life and the existence of spiritual reality. The body is the great unknown. We have no idea when it will fall ill, or when it will die. It should come as no surprise, then, that many of our deep-rooted fears about disease, death, and the uncertainties of life are funneled into our relationship to food and nutrition. We search for the perfect diet that will make our bodies immortal, therapeutic foods that will purge us of toxins and leave us disease-free, or psychological techniques that will give us control of the unpredictable features of bodily life—weight gain, binges, cravings, and desires.

Of course, it is important to explore the best foods for one's body and the nutritional philosophies that seem most suited for one's way of thinking. But without a spiritual foundation, nutritional knowledge can go only so far. Science can tell us what to eat, but it cannot pronounce upon the *meaning* of eating. We need something more to help us understand the richness, drama, emotions, sensuousness, and psychological significance of eating.

Food is the soul's earliest experience of miracles. A crying baby is transformed into a calm and satisfied one with a little mother's milk. And a miserable child can change into a creative, playful force with a helping of the right food. Children eat naturally and spontaneously, without fear and without concepts of what should or should not be eaten. They certainly have their preferences, but unlike adults they experience little guilt and make no judgments about the eating habits of others. Children eat because they enjoy eating.

As we grow older we lose some of the child within. Of necessity we move from the primordial bliss of childhood to the separateness of adulthood. In the process our connectedness to the universe and the timeless nature of the soul fade to a dim memory, and we begin to feel isolated and alone. Eventually our relationship to food changes.

As adults we eat food not to nourish ourselves, but to avoid pain, loneliness, and depression. We adopt beliefs about the right and wrong foods to eat and stand in judgment of anyone—including ourselves—who eats "incorrectly." The mind busily chews on its fears and fantasies about food, and we miss the experience of joyous eating in the present moment. With the spontaneity of the inner child all but forgotten, we eat with the mind rather than with our body and being.

Few are content to live in such confusion for long. We search for a way to eat that feels "right," a nutrition that makes the body hum and the soul sing. This search begins when we admit we have little control over our habits, and that as eaters we can be so much more. We realize our relationship to food can serve as a vehicle through which we can learn about our relationship to life.

Each of us uses food or other popular substances to play out our hunger for the spiritual source. Alcoholics express the hunger for the Divine through alcohol, an anorexic or bulemic expresses it through food, and a drug addict through drugs. The expression of this longing need not be a problematic one. It may just as easily show up as a *celebration* of life through these same pastimes.

No substance is inherently bad or evil. It is the way we use a substance that determines its value. A knife can be used to cut vegetables or kill the innocent. An attack victim will look at a knife and see a weapon, while a chef will see something quite different. The knife is neutral. It is we who ascribe to it a label and a value. The same is true of food.

In the past we have assigned food certain moral values. For instance, we may have concluded that sugar was evil or meat was bad. Labeling food in this way automatically sets up a cycle of perpetual anxiety, for once we label something bad, we invariably desire it, and the desire grows stronger the more we resist the food. Consequently we label *ourselves* bad for having the desire, which results in the guilt we experience when eating forbidden foods.

By giving power to food rather than seeing things as they really are, we feel helpless and weak in the body. We are afraid of sugar, overeating, and any food or desire we have labeled bad. Consequently, our dignity, centeredness, and rootedness in the physical form are lost. Is sugar really something one should fear? Is a cookie so threatening that it is best left hidden in the cupboard?

In this state of confused reality where food has power, where the spiritual source is forgotten, and where the threat of death and disease lingers in the subconscious mind, it seems as if the body is all we have and that we must use it to fight our imaginary foes. We ask questions such as, How can I gain control over food? How can I master my emotions and desires? and How can I find the perfect diet to end all my worries? Many people spend a lifetime searching for these answers, but we can never find the right answers if we are asking the wrong questions.

Placing the search for nutritional enlightenment within the larger search for spiritual enlightenment, we begin to ask the questions that matter most: Who am I? Why am I here? What is the nature of life? What do I aspire to? What is the ultimate purpose of feeding my body? How can I best nourish myself? Is there more to food than just nutrients? Can I learn to value my body and find joy in eating? How does my relationship to food reveal how I relate to the world?

Each time you eat, know that you are feeding more than just a body. You are feeding the soul's longing for life, its timeless desire to learn the lessons of earthly existence—love and hate, pleasure and pain, fear and faith, illusion and truth—through the vehicle of food. Ultimately, the most important aspect of nutrition is not what to eat but how our relationship to food can teach us who we are and how we can sustain ourselves at the deepest level of being.

## KEY LESSONS

- We are more than just a body; we are of a spiritual source.
- By nourishing the body, we nourish the spark of life within the body.
- The body is sacred and, therefore, the nutrition of the body is sacred.
- A truly evolved nutritional approach takes us fully *into* the body and *beyond* the body.
- Our relationship to food teaches us a great deal about who we are and how we live.

## REFLECTIONS

- How does your relationship to food obstruct awareness of your spiritual nature?
- How can food serve as a reminder of your spiritual nature?
- If you had only one week to live, how would your relationship to food and to your body change?
- If you were reborn tomorrow, what advice would you give yourself about your relationship to food and nourishment? How could you use that advice now?

# 2

# Changing Body, Changing Diet

The questions I hear most often about diet are, What should I eat? Which is the best diet to follow? Behind these questions is the assumption that there *is* a perfect diet, and all one need do is discover it. But consider for a moment the implications of a perfect diet. Perfection implies sameness. If we all followed the perfect religion, everyone would think and act similarly. If each of us drove the perfect car or had the perfect job, we would all be parking and working in the same place. Likewise, if everyone ate the one perfect diet, we would all be eating the same food.

The most telling characteristic of the perfect diet is the hidden assumption that the body remains unchanged and has the same nutritional needs at every stage of development. But, as we know, nothing could be further from reality. If there is any guarantee that comes with living in a body, it is change. Each second ten million red blood cells are born and die. The stomach lining completely regenerates in a week, a healthy liver in six weeks, and the skin surface in a month. Scientists postulate that 98 percent of all atoms in the body are replaced within a year, 100 percent within seven years.*

From the time of conception to the flowering of adulthood, the body grows from one cell to one quadrillion cells (1,000,000,000,000,000). Total body weight may increase twentyfold to sixtyfold from birth, while brain size, muscle mass, percent of body fat, and bone density increase (or decrease) at their own particular rates.

Even within the course of a day the body undergoes a wide range of physiological changes. It rhythmically shifts in temperature, metabolic rate, respiratory function, brain wave patterns, endorphin production, serum nutrient levels, hormonal and enzymatic production, and energy output.

Perhaps the most noticeable changes in the body occur in health. We move through an endless parade of aches, pains, coughs, colds, tensions, and sensitivities along with periods of relative health and high energy. With all these changes in the body, does it not make sense that our nutritional needs change? A single diet could not possibly keep pace with those changes.

A changing body means a changing diet. You have not had just one body in this life—you have had many—and each of these bodies has called for a different way to eat. Consider the dramatic shift that occurs in the life of a newborn as it makes the transition from umbilical-cord nourishment to breast or bottle. No longer is its nutritive process a passive one through the belly. It must actively reach for milk and for the first time carry out the function of digestion completely on its own. The introduction of solid food marks yet another important tran-

*Although there are cells in the body such as certain types of brain cells that may last a lifetime and never regenerate to their original functional capacity when destroyed, the *atoms* in the cells are nevertheless continually replaced.

sition for the child. Its body is growing at a rapid rate, and its digestive system must meet a completely new set of challenges in breaking down and assimilating complex molecular foodstuffs.

No one complains to an infant that it is getting too much fat in its diet—mother's milk is 52 percent fat—or that it needs a wider variety of foods. For its particular physiology and activity level, it is eating the perfect diet. And yet that perfect diet will change. The infant may grow to be an active toddler, a high-school athlete, a health-food-eating college student, an office worker, a parent, a partygoer, or an invalid, with each of these different "bodies" calling for its own special nutrition.

## The Changing Diet: Five Key Factors

There are five key factors that influence the changing nature of the body and hence the diet: life-style, environment, season, age, and health. These factors continually interact to form a new picture of our emotional and biological needs.

### LIFE-STYLE

Think for a moment of the times when your life-style changed—a move to a new location, a different job or career, a shift in finances, or a change in your exercise level, sleep schedule, or recreational pursuits. Did your body have different needs? Did it change in noticeable ways? Were you drawn to different foods?

A changing life-style means a changing diet. For example, if you are working at a desk all day, physical exertion is minimized, metabolism decreases, and caloric needs drop. In other words, you require less food. If you switched to a landscaping or construction job, caloric and nutrient needs would automatically rise and your appetite would increase. Body chemistry is dramatically altered simply by switching jobs.

People working in a high-stress environment or a boring job might find themselves hungrier than usual; food serves either to calm us down or activate our interest when we feel unfulfilled. The same person who is wholeheartedly engaged and 100 percent involved in his or her job might not feel hungry for hours. People who love their job often report they have less desire for food because they are so nourished and energized by their work. Can you recall an instance when you were so absorbed in an activity that you were not hungry at mealtime?

Life-style changes also include exercise level and type. A marathon runner has different nutritional needs from a weekend jogger, while anyone training for endurance has different needs from those training for strength. Current research strongly suggests that even a moderate amount of exercise done regularly can alter metabolism and affect the rate at which we digest food, burn fat, and build muscle. People often report that upon adopting a type of exercise they have never done before or simply including any exercise into a sedentary life-style, they begin to crave certain foods. Those who begin weightlifting often desire high protein foods, particularly meat and fish. One woman who took up bicycling started to crave oatmeal cookies and bananas, and another woman who began aerobic walking *lost* her intense cravings for coffee and sugar.

A change in our daily schedule also brings about changes in body and diet. Many people who switch to a late night schedule or work a "graveyard shift" report digestive discomfort, weight gain, and an assortment of minor health complaints—headaches, joint pains, and grogginess. Research has revealed that digestive capacity is highest at noon, which corresponds to the hottest time of the day. Reversing our schedule so that we eat a big meal in the late evening, when digestive metabolism is at its lowest level, is a challenge to the inherent rhythms of the digestive system and naturally creates disorders in the body.

I have noted with great fascination the influence of life-style on my diet. When I was a medical student, time seemed more valuable than anything in the world, so the last thing I wanted to do was cook. I ate out twice a day, three times if you consider that breakfast was often last night's leftovers. My diet was unusually limited because I found only two restaurants in Syracuse—a Greek restaurant and a small Mexican take-out place—that were cheap, convenient, and served what I enjoyed. For an entire year my diet consisted of falafel, chick-pea salad, bean burritos, and orange juice.

My life-style determined my diet, which in turn influenced the health of my body. I experienced chronic gas problems and stomachaches caused by the oily food, felt sluggish after meals, and was gaining weight even though I was eating less food than before. The cold weather of upstate New York coupled with my busy schedule made it difficult to exercise, and my metabolism simply slowed down.

Leaving school and moving to Southern California marked a dramatic shift. I worked as a free-lance sales manager for several health-food and vitamin companies and naturally grew more health conscious. I had little stress, plenty of free time, and lived in a beach community in San Diego where everyone seemed to exercise, sun themselves, and eat papayas. I rediscovered my body, taking long ocean swims and playing Frisbee in the park.

I also rediscovered my love for food. I ate from an abundance of locally grown fruits and vegetables, preparing fresh meals each day, and experimenting with new foods like guacamole or tofu sandwiches. Any desire for falafel or bean burritos was gone. I felt light and energized, my digestive problems disappeared, and I lost the weight gained in Syracuse even though I was eating more.

Five years later a move to New York City brought yet another life-style change. The bathing suit was replaced by a business suit. Working as a marketing and public relations consultant for food and vitamin companies, I had deadlines to meet and subways to catch. Lunch was now a "business lunch." I was not so much concerned with *what* I ate as with *whom* I ate. I would agree to whichever restaurant my client preferred and would order food I normally would not choose—sushi, asparagus tips in lime vinaigrette, and buffalo mozzarella.

Even more dramatic was my shift in eating schedule. New York City time was different from anywhere I had been before. I would often eat dinner late at night and have breakfast at 11:00 A.M. My body felt heavy and congested in the morning, and even though I got up at 7:30 A.M., I did not really wake up until hours later. Rather than the sense of vibrancy I felt in California, I experienced a sense of urgency—my body felt as if it needed either stimulation to work or sedation to recover from work.

Though I knew about good nutrition, the life I was leading took precedence over the foods I thought I should be eating. It was as if my job, my apartment, and my hectic schedule *were* the nutrition I needed most, and the food itself was secondary.

## ENVIRONMENT

Environment is another important influence in our changing body and diet. People often report that upon moving to a new location they desire foods indigenous to that environment. One woman from South Carolina moved to Key West, Florida, and instantly developed an appetite for tropical fruit.

Another woman moved to Sebastopol, California, one of the primary apple-producing regions in the country, and developed a keen taste for anything apple—juice, sauce, or pie— despite a previous distaste for apples.

When I moved to Southern California I began a love affair with avocados. I had tasted avocados only once before and found them unpalatable, yet something about San Diego made avocados taste good. They grew in backyards, in small orchards, and on trees lining residential streets. Avocados were in the air, and breathing where they were grown made me long for more of them.

When I moved to New York City my avocado affair ended and my pizza phase began. For five years in California I ate a "pizzaless" diet. Even to think about pizza made my stomach turn. The heat of Southern California plus my attraction to a diet centered around fruits and vegetables simply made pizza unappealing.

The moment I stepped onto Manhattan concrete, something inside me changed. No longer was I living in spacious, relaxed California. The New York City sidewalks were crowded and electric, and I felt as though something was needed to anchor me in the flood of activity. Pizza was that something. Certainly, this was not a deliberate, well-thought-out plan on my part. Yet somehow I found my way into a pizza place and then surprised myself by digesting four slices with ease. Despite a previous belief that pizza was bad for my body, it became a staple food for over a year.

Was my desire for avocados in San Diego or pizza in New York City psychological? Did these desires have a biological basis? Or were both components present? To each of these questions I would answer an emphatic yes.

An intimate connection exists between the food native to a region and the people living there. In the study of any ecosystem the organisms within a biological community are integrally linked to the available sources of food. It is not uncommon for animals to move into a new biological niche or territory—whether through population or environmental pressures—and adapt to new foods. Though human beings are not fully bound by the same natural laws as animals—we make psychological food choices more than biological ones—we still remain connected to our surroundings in tangible ways.

Eating the food unique to a given environment *joins* us to that environment. Just as an old house contains the memories and personalities of the generations that lived there, so too does food contain the essence of its environment. The heart, soul, and character of the land lie within its food.

Of course, pizza is not "indigenous" to New York City, yet for me it was the staple crop. Pizza meant Manhattan. I was not just eating a high-fat, high-protein food that gave me a sustained caloric burn and a grounded sensation in my mid-section. I was swallowing up the Empire State Building, Greenwich Village, Lincoln Center, and the hidden dreams of every aspiring actor, writer, dancer, or entrepreneur. And in San Diego I was not just eating avocados, a food filled with vitamin A, unsaturated fats, and essential minerals, I was consuming the whole atmosphere—the warm desert winds, the tropical fruit trees, the jugglers in Balboa Park, and volleyball on the beach.

Diet, then, is a function of our environment. As our surroundings change, we change. Of course these dietary changes have a strong personal component: we are influenced by the people, the culture, and the excitement of a new environment. But are our biological needs entirely separate from our personal needs? Could there be a place where the two needs merge and nourish us more deeply than either by itself?

## SEASON

Closely related to environmental changes are seasonal ones. Seasonal cycles exert a profound influence on the needs of the body. For example, body metabolism and temperature normally increase simply by eating food, hence the old adage, Feed a cold and starve a fever. During the hot spring and summer months the sun's energy warms the body, and we have less need to produce internal heat through the digestive process, so our appetite naturally decreases.

In addition, hot seasonal temperatures stimulate increased perspiration—the body's mechanism for cooling itself—and hence our need for more fluid to replace the water lost through the skin. Many people recognize this as an increased thirst for cool liquids in the summertime and a corresponding decrease in the desire for hot foods. The environment graciously supports these changes in the body through the availability of fruits and vegetables in the warm seasons, the foods most naturally high in water content. Interestingly, even though metabolism increases in the warmer months, it is often slowed by extremely high temperatures. You may have had the experience of feeling energized in the spring but lethargic in the heat of the summer. Hence the custom of eating hot spicy foods in hot-weather climates such as curry in India or chili peppers in Mexico, which increases body metabolism and perspiration.

Conversely, metabolism decreases in the wintertime as body temperature mechanisms are challenged by the cold. Appetite naturally increases at this time as the body yearns for greater caloric intake to help keep its temperature within a normal range. Most people recognize this as a desire for hot foods and soups in the wintertime and an attraction to high-fat and high-protein foods such as meats, cheeses, casseroles, and fried foods. These foods are high in calories, take longer to digest than fruits and vegetables, and yield a sustained heat release in the body over a longer period of time.

Not only does the body call for more food in the winter months, it also calls for more weight, particularly body fat. Researchers have discovered that body weight is generally greatest when the mean January temperature is lowest. This extra body fat is an evolutionary adaptation to insulate us from the cold and provide an emergency source of caloric energy.

## AGE

Age is another factor influencing our changing dietary needs. In the course of only a few years the perfect diet changes from umbilical-cord nourishment to breast milk to simple puréed food. Then the body longs for more complex foods to challenge the digestive system into full function and to meet the child's growing nutritional needs. It is a miracle that within such a brief time the process of nourishment alters in so many profound ways.

The transformation of body and diet continues into adulthood. You may have noticed the huge amount of food teenagers consume or remember your own ravenous appetite in adolescence. The rate at which a teenage body grows and metabolizes demands a larger amount of food per pound of body weight relative to other age groups.

On the other hand, you may have noticed the small amounts of food many elderly people consume. Because of their decreased rate of metabolism, they need only a fraction of the calories required to maintain a similar size youth. The decrease in metabolism and physical output is why many elderly people can eat small amounts of food and gain weight. Other age-related changes in senior citizens include decreased taste sensation, decreased nutrient needs, and even a drop in the psychological desire for food.

Medical science has certainly focused on the unique nutritional needs of the young and the old, but the ages between twenty and fifty-five are generally clumped together in one homogeneous group. What are the differences in nutritional requirements between a twenty- and a thirty-year-old? Between a forty- and a fifty-year-old? These distinctions are subtle, yet much remains to be uncovered in this area. In the meantime, suffice it to say that age changes lead to body changes, which lead to diet changes.

## HEALTH

Health is the last key factor influencing diet. Many of us are accustomed to adjusting our diet during common illnesses such as colds, flu, and fever, and during undiagnosed health conditions such as low energy episodes, digestive complaints, or periods of low immunity. The foods we choose may be unusually bland or spicy, appetite may fluctuate, or we may reach for favorite food remedies—teas, soups, fruits, toast, and so on.

For some people health considerations alter diet for life. Special diets are crucial during chronic illnesses such as heart disease, liver disease, diabetes, and ulcers. Each of these medical conditions has a corresponding therapeutic diet with specific food guidelines to support or perhaps even heal the body.

For a diabetic the perfect diet is low in sugar and high in complex carbohydrates. For those with gout, a low-meat, low-protein diet proves best, while heart disease patients follow a low-fat, high-fiber regime. Other special body states such as pregnancy, lactation, and menstruation also have unique nutritional considerations.

Can you see how the five key factors—life-style, environment, season, age, and health—interact to create a ceaselessly changing diet? Do you still think it's possible for a single, perfect diet to exist?

The body symbolizes that which is changing, ephemeral, and beyond control. Though we seldom ponder our destination, all sentient beings intuit the body's ultimate fate—death and disintegration. Because we fear the uncertain nature of death *and* the uncertain nature of life, we attempt to control the unknown by controlling the body.

By following a diet we believe to be perfect, we are pretending that the body never changes and that we can therefore avoid the unknown. Have you noticed how often we do not act upon a decision until we are certain of the outcome? Believing in a perfect diet means we need not worry about nutritional changes that might otherwise perplex us. Our cookbook tells us what to do and keeps our diet free from any surprises. And yet, when the body undergoes inevitable change and yearns for foods outside this "perfect system," we experience great conflict. We believe something is wrong with us because we cannot hold to our imagined standards of perfection.

The fear of shifting to new foods as the body's needs fluctuate is symbolic of our fear of change—change in our job, health, family, relationships, or inner consciousness. Life moves from the known to the unknown. Whether it is discoveries in science, the outcome of a baseball game, tomorrow's weather, or next minute's mood, we can never be certain of what is next. Even if we could know something for sure, say, that we will have a telephone conversation with a friend at an agreed time, we still do not know how we will react in that instant. This moment is known; the next moment is unknown.

Believing that a perfect diet will protect us from the unknown changes in the body is like buying an insurance policy from an imaginary company; it never pays off. Rather than search for the ideal way to eat, allow yourself to find the answers by dropping the questions altogether, at least for a little while. I am deliberately staying away from nutritional advice and guidelines for now because you can find nutritional information almost anywhere. Nutritional *wisdom*, though, is rare.

The claims for optimum foods and nutrients have been greatly overstated in the printed media. I am overstating another approach—not the science of eating but the consciousness of eating, the awareness necessary to examine the basis of our scientific beliefs, nutritional biases, and emotional relationship with eating. For, in the long run, understanding the mind of the eater may well prove to be as nourishing an act as understanding the foods that are best to eat.

## KEY LESSONS

- There is no single, perfect way to eat. Diet changes as the body changes.

- Because we fear changes in the body and the inevitability of disease and death, we try to take control by believing in a perfect diet that guarantees perpetual health.

- The fear of shifting to new foods with the body's changing needs is symbolic of our fears about adjusting to changes in life.

- Diet is an ongoing process of learning and discovery.

## REFLECTIONS

- What is the purpose of change? Why is it useful?

- How have changes in your life-style affected your diet? What specific foods have you included or excluded with changes in your work, exercise level, sleep schedule, religious practice, or recreational pursuits?

- Can you recall instances when a change in living environment precipitated changes in diet? What were the specific dietary changes?

- Have you noticed your body changing with the different seasons? Are there specific foods you are drawn to as the seasons progress? How do these foods affect you? Does your appetite level change with the seasons? Your liquid intake? Your eating schedule?

- Can you visualize the dietary transformations in your life as they relate to age? What were your different sources of food?

- Does your diet shift as your health changes? Are there particular foods you faithfully eat when you are ill?

- Do any particular states of mind predominate when your diet needs to shift—eagerness, poise, resistance, fear, uncertainty? Are there adjustments in attitude you can make or practical steps you can take to enable yourself to adapt better to dietary changes?

- Has your changing diet been accompanied by changes in personality or level of awareness? Do you notice any connections between what you eat and how you see the world?

# 3

# *The Spectrum of Nutrition*

If no perfect diet exists, you may wonder why so many different dietary systems claim to be the best. A well-stocked bookstore may have as many as thirty different titles in the health and nutrition section, each written by a medical doctor, research scientist, or nutrition expert, and every one prescribing a different way to eat. What is more intriguing, most of these books contain solid scientific evidence to prove the superiority of their diets.

For example, raw foods enthusiasts promote raw fruits and vegetables and sprouted grains as the ultimate way to eat and provide documented case studies in which patients with an assortment of debilitating or life-threatening diseases have been miraculously cured under the supervision of respected medical doctors. They cite laboratory research that validates what has already been clinically demonstrated—that a raw foods diet indeed works.

Next, traditional* macrobiotic practitioners dispute nearly every principle a raw foods diet is based upon, claiming their own version of specially cooked and prepared foods works best, and that only about 5 percent of raw foods in the diet is well tolerated. And, of course, they present a battery of well-documented case studies that clearly validate the healing powers of a macrobiotic diet along with the necessary scientific theory, each theory quite different from those presented by raw foods advocates.

If this is not confusing enough for the rational scientific mind, then consider the example of a well-known doctor in New York City who espouses a predominantly meat-centered, high-protein diet and has used this approach successfully as a therapeutic intervention for certain cancer patients. Not only does this go against every alternative system of nutrition, it even contradicts the current findings in mainstream science on the dangers of excessive amounts of animal food in the diet.

Over the years I have had clinical contact with patients on each of these diets in addition to several others—wheatgrass-juice-and-sprout diets, the Pritikin program, and Gerson therapy—and have observed clearcut success in each. How can this possibly make sense? How can one set of medical results prove macrobiotics work, another set prove raw fruits and vegetables works, and yet more scientific documentation prove the healing power of lean meats? Are people lying? Is there a way to make sense of the success of all the different nutritional approaches?

If you have asked these questions before, allow me to save you over thirty years of work by summing it up in this way:

---

*Note that there is a distinction between "traditional" macrobiotics, which is very specific in scope, and "contemporary" macrobiotics, which is broader in its use of different foods.

There is no single perfect diet but many. Different dietary systems are effective for different people under different circumstances.

Scattered across the earth are people of vastly different races, cultures, body types, and belief systems. They live near mountains, oceans, rivers, deserts, tundra, tropics, forests, and flatlands. Some have only fish and a few varieties of plants available to eat, some an assortment of tropical fruits and vegetables, some have only yak milk, meat, and a little grain, while others have enough fertile land and resources to raise crops, herd animals, and mass-produce every imaginable variety of food.

Is it sensible for any one people to tell another about the "true" way to eat? Can a tribesman from West Africa whose staple food is cassava root tell an Eskimo he is wrong because his staple food is fish? Or can the Japanese tell the Mexicans of the absurdity of eating dairy, corn, hot peppers, and food fried in lard, staple products completely unknown to native Japan?

The most cursory study of evolution reveals that there is not merely one but a whole spectrum of nutritional systems suitable for human consumption. This spectrum of nutrition is inherently diverse and is a function of genetic inheritance (the unique biological characteristics of the different races), geography (the environment in which the foods are grown), and cultural beliefs (the unique ways in which various ethnic groups across the globe see the universe). These elements compose the nutritional code of ethics for a given people.

Most dietary experts fail to notice the full range of nutrition or simply disclaim the legitimacy of other diets. They see things only from the perspective of their own limited viewpoint. This is not unlike people who have had life-changing religious experiences and conclude that because they have found spiritual meaning through a particular religious tradition, you should too. Theirs is the only path to salvation and failure to follow it spells spiritual doom.

## Reading the Body

Whenever a nutrition scientist or medical expert champions a particular diet, or when someone who has found success with a nutritional approach wholeheartedly endorses it as the only way to eat, what they are doing is reading their body and translating it onto yours. They make the assumption that because a diet worked for them, it *must* work for you. This assumption will hold true only as far as your body type, health characteristics, and life-style needs are similar to theirs.

For example, many nutrition experts extoll the use of dairy products, seeing them as essential. Indeed, they work well for many people. However, certain African and Oriental ethnic groups have a curious intolerance for milk products. Researchers have discovered that these groups have a low concentration of lactase, the enzyme that breaks down the milk sugar lactose. Dairy products were unknown to their ancestors, and hence many Africans and Orientals are genetically less well adapted to digest milk than, say, their Indo-European counterparts whose ancestors depended on dairy for survival.

It is quite natural for someone with a high lactase concentration to conclude that dairy products are easy to digest and necessary for good health. It is equally likely for those with a low lactase level who experience gas and stomach cramps when drinking milk to conclude that dairy products are "bad." However, neither of these conclusions is useful if it is generalized.

What is more fascinating, many people of eastern European descent who have a high lactase concentration nevertheless show an unusual sensitivity to dairy products. In clinical settings I have observed people who have complained for decades of clogged sinuses, postnasal drip, and sinus headaches only to have the condition clear dramatically after eliminating all dairy products from the diet for several weeks. Once again, dairy products are not bad food; they simply work well for some body types and poorly for others.

In another example some nutritional systems, such as strict vegetarian (no meat, fish, or dairy), Pritikin, macrobiotics, and raw foods, advocate a diet high in carbohydrates and low in protein and fat as compared with standard American fare. These diets may indeed work well for people with smaller body frames, less lean body tissue, or slower metabolism; however, those with larger frames, more muscle tissue, and physically active life-styles often lose weight, feel less fulfilled, and simply cannot sustain themselves on these diets.

## Body Phases

Proponents of different nutritional systems not only read their body *type* but also their body *phase* and erroneously translate these to other people. In certain Eastern and European esoteric healing traditions, the body is characterized as cyclically passing through three distinct phases: cleansing, building, and sustaining.

The cleansing phase is a period of "breaking down," a time when it feels as if the body is at its weakest level of function. We may be experiencing illness, low immunity, low energy, depressed mood, or decreased appetite and weight loss. A cleansing phase is the body's time to purify, a purging of toxic elements on the biological level and a housecleaning of outdated habits on the emotional level. The cleansing body actively sheds toxins by focusing energy on catabolic processes, or the breakdown of diseased tissues. This tearing away of tissue is a necessary step for the phase that follows next—building.

The building phase is a time of growth, a flowering season for the body. During this phase the body metabolizes at its greatest efficiency, rebuilding anew that which was torn down in the cleansing process. Organ systems strengthen, immune function is enhanced, and body weight may increase. People often experience a building phase as a period of increased appetite, enhanced digestion, mood elevation, high energy, and a general feeling of strength and earthiness. It is as if we were becoming "more" of ourself, re-creating the body.

In the sustaining phase the body operates on a maintenance level. This is a period of functional stasis when metabolic processes are balanced between the polar opposites of cleansing and building. Many people experience the sustaining phase as a time of evenness in body and temperament, a feeling that we are operating on "cruise control."

The three phases are not limited to the human body. Every creature and plant, every natural phenomenon from snowstorms to volcanic eruptions to planetary orbits move through periods of increase, stasis, and decay. As far as I can tell, an inherent mechanism orchestrates the timing of the movement from cleansing to building to sustaining in the body; however, the onset and duration of these phases along with their relative "success" are not absolutely set. They are influenced by a host of factors, the most important of which is diet.

Different nutritional systems enhance one particular phase more than the others, sometimes in dramatic fashion. For example, a raw foods diet steers the body into a cleansing state, causing the breakdown of diseased tissues and the release of stored toxins. If you undertake a raw foods diet while the body is already in a cleansing state, or ready to move into one (for instance in the early spring when we naturally shed excess fatty tissue accumulated in the winter), the diet may have profound effects. Illness and pains may vanish, stores of energy be released, and a wonderful clarity of mind appear.

Those who have this experience correctly perceive the healing effect of the diet but often incorrectly conclude that the diet works all the time and for all bodies. Your body may not be in a cleansing phase when you read a book on raw foods dieting or receive counseling from a medical practitioner who emphasizes this diet. Indeed, once someone on a raw foods regime is ready to move from the cleansing to building phase, staying on the raw foods diet may have disquieting effects. The body wants to move in one direction, but the diet is pulling it back in another direction. The results of this dietary "push me–pull you" may be irritability, physical hypersensitivity, cravings, excessive weight loss, and constant hunger.

What is more, many people who follow a year-round raw foods regimen meet with relative success because they live in hot weather or tropical locations like Hawaii, Florida, or Southern California—environments that naturally support the cleansing process. Try eating raw fruits and vegetables for twelve months in Montana and you will learn firsthand why it does not always work.

A traditional macrobiotic diet is basically a sustaining diet for Oriental bodies; it maintains the body without steering it toward a cleansing or building state. For many westerners, however, I have found a macrobiotic diet yields a "sustained cleanse." The same cleansing effect that occurs in two weeks on a raw foods diet may take months on a macrobiotic diet. Many westerners who follow this diet experience feelings of calm, balance, and stability along with increased energy and remission of a long list of pathologies.

Those who continue the diet past the sustaining and cleansing phases, however, often lose weight, appear gaunt, and experience energy drops, hunger pangs, and cravings for meat, fish, and dairy products. They have chosen a diet that supports a portion of the body's changing needs, but they fail to recognize the nutritional demands of the building period. And by falsely reading their bodies as existing in a state of perpetual "sustained cleanse," many traditional macrobiotic experts assume all other bodies are similar to theirs. The precise reasons why a macrobiotic diet works well for some westerners and not others is not yet understood. Suffice it to say that it is the nuances of individual body type and body chemistry that ultimately determine the effectiveness of a diet over a long period of time.

In general, a diet high in meat and animal products initially steers the body toward a building phase. These foods help promote weight increase, tissue regeneration, and other anabolic functions. Those who follow a diet high in animal foods often report feelings of strength, solidity, and fulfillment of appetite, particularly when the body is already in a building period. Once the body enters the cleansing phase, the further use of animal foods inhibits the body from fully investing energy in the process of tearing down and healing dysfunctional tissue. The energy needed to digest animal foods and excrete their toxic by-products places too large a demand on the system.

I am certainly aware that not all those who follow the diets I have listed see from such a limited perspective and that there are indeed elegant variations of macrobiotic and raw foods diets that adjust for the imbalances I have listed. I have mentioned these general examples to clarify a fine point: Any scientist or layperson may experience success with a diet that supports a particular body phase and falsely conclude that the diet works for all bodies all the time.

## Eat My System

There is still more to the story. Whenever people passionately promote a nutritional system, they are not just asking you to swallow certain foods, they are asking you to accept the worldview on which the diet is based. A "dietary philosophy" is exactly that—a diet based upon a larger philosophy of how the universe works.

By telling you to avoid meat, for example, some vegetarian proponents are not only asking you to eliminate it because it is harmful to health, they are telling you to "eat my system, eat my way of seeing the world, eat my belief that killing animals is unhealthy for your soul, and that abstaining from meat will make you a better person." Likewise, when meat eaters tell you to eat meat, they are not just promoting its health-giving effects, they are saying "eat my system, eat my belief that it is acceptable to kill animals, that eating meat does not make you morally corrupt."

People could argue for days about whose nutritional system is most correct, but they are not so much trying to validate a system of nutrition as a system of thinking. Ultimately, nutritional experts are not only saying "eat like me," they are saying "think like me."

A macrobiotic diet, for example, is not merely a way to eat, it is a way to live. Macrobiotic principles form a richly articulated worldview that includes one's relationship to spiritual, social, and biological realities. A student of macrobiotics can study for years to learn the principles of macrobiotic *living* on which the system of macrobiotic *eating* is based.

Furthermore, many nutritional systems are based not upon what is good for the body's health, but what is believed to be good for the soul's health. For example, various traditional schools of vegetarianism and raw foods have their roots in religious movements that developed strict moral codes about behavior. Any foods that stimulated the "passions of the body" were considered taboo. In fact, one of the first nutritional spokespersons in America—a Presbyterian minister named Sylvester Graham (of graham cracker fame)—supported the use of whole wheat flour and fresh fruits and vegetables not so much for health purposes, but because he believed foods such as meat, fish, eggs, spices, and liquor stimulated the sex drive and should be stricken from the diet. He was not trying to make healthier people, he was trying to make better people.

Even someone who follows no formal nutritional system is nevertheless operating upon a larger belief system on which the "nondiet" is based. For example, many people who want no rules or restrictions with diet and believe "anything goes" with eating often operate on the belief that no relationship exists between cause and effect. Somehow, whatever they do in life or whatever they eat will not have future consequences, or so they hope. Because they secretly fear responsibility, they act as if responsibility were unnecessary.

## Different Systems, Different Diagnoses

It is fascinating to observe how practitioners of different nutritional systems arrive at such diverse diagnoses. One person I know had a long-term digestive disorder that caused gas, stomach cramps, and intestinal pains whenever he ate. He jumped from one nutritional therapy to another, ultimately giving up in confusion at the different approaches.

An allergy doctor diagnosed his condition (not surprisingly) as food allergies, and placed him on a rotation diet, eliminating most of his favorite foods and placing him on a regimen that consisted of 50 percent raw salads. Disappointed in the diet, he turned to a Chinese doctor who diagnosed his condition as deficiency of "warmth," and prescribed warming spices—ginger and garlic to help heal the intestines. He also emphasized that little or no salad should be eaten.

When this diet failed, he consulted an Ayurvedic physician from India who told him the opposite: He had too much warmth in his system, and it was best to avoid warming spices, particularly ginger and garlic. He was also told to avoid salt because it heats the system and to include more sweets because they soothe the digestive system.

When this approach showed no improvement, he consulted a macrobiotic counselor who diagnosed his condition as overly yin (expansive) and prescribed more salt because it contracts the system, and fewer sweets because they expand the system—the opposite prescription given by the Ayurvedic doctor. Unlike the Chinese approach that uses spices to heal the digestive system, spices are avoided in the macrobiotic worldview because they obstruct digestion. Eventually he tired of his search and decided to let the problem alone until another avenue emerged. In the interim he took up bicycling and within a month's time the condition was halfway cleared.

I consider none of these systems to be right or wrong. Each has a unique worldview on which its nutritional philosophy is based, and even though they directly contradict each other in certain areas, each approach will still work for certain people under the right conditions. Indeed, one of the most important success-promoting factors in a diet is a belief in the diet and a belief in the belief system behind the diet.

## The Problem of Proof

We are often confused, and rightfully so, when different nutritionists offer scientific proof of their particular viewpoints. How can one scientist prove raw foods are best and another prove cooked foods? How can one set of scientific results demonstrate that excess sodium raises blood pressure and another study show it lowers pressure? The answer lies in the *interpretation* of scientific results. The renegade philosopher Robert Anton Wilson has pointed out that the mind often behaves as if it has two parts: the thinker and the prover. Whatever the thinker thinks, the prover sets out to prove. In other words, scientists make interpretations based on personal biases, just as any of us would interpret a situation from our own unique viewpoint.

Some studies shows a direct link between cholesterol in the diet and cholesterol level in the blood, but other studies show no correlation at all. Some studies demonstrate the effectiveness of vitamin C in preventing colds and others show its ineffectiveness. There are even scientists (hired by tobacco companies) who claim there is no conclusive evidence linking cigarette smoking to lung disease, even though more research has been amassed to prove that there *is* than perhaps any medical condition. And when a majority of scientists agree, someone always dissents, and that voice is often a Galileo, a Newton, or an Einstein who dares to see differently. The problem of proof arises when we believe our interpretation of evidence is the *only* interpretation of the evidence.

For example, raw foods enthusiasts point to scientific evidence which shows that when cooked foods are consumed, the white blood cell count immediately rises, while no such increase occurs when eating raw fruits or vegetables. The white blood cells function as immune system scavengers, removing foreign organisms and any chemical compounds the body considers invasive. The conclusion is drawn that therefore cooked foods are bad because the body considers them invasive and toxic, and raw foods are good because they evoke no immune system response. However, one can look at the same results and conclude that the cooked food is *stimulating* the immune function and causing the increase in white blood cells not because the food itself is toxic, but because a function of cooked food is to "exercise" the immune system in producing white blood cells for real emergencies, somewhat akin to a biological fire drill. Indeed, it is quite natural for the body to use the invasion of low doses of microorganisms or chemical poisons to immunize itself against greater danger. And on one level food *is* a foreign substance that the body must "overcome" through the process of digestion and assimilation. In this sense cooked food can be seen to strengthen the system while raw foods simply do not have the same white-blood-cell-stimulating effect.

In another example one scientist I know was interested in proving a vegetarian diet biologically inferior. His studies of the digestive system revealed the existence of a carrier molecule in the bloodstream that transports the type of iron found only in animal foods. In other words, the iron from meat is in a different chemically bound form from the iron in plants, and the subjects he tested had special, previously unknown chemicals that carried only the animal or "heme-bound" form of iron. He concluded that because this carrier protein exists, human beings were therefore meant to eat meat. This reasoning is certainly logical, but one could just as readily conclude that because one eats meat, special iron-carrying proteins are produced in the body to accommodate meat's unique form of iron. Indeed, his subjects were all meat-eaters; none were vegetarian. Who knows what he would have found if he had tested both these groups? Trying to prove what we were "meant" to eat is ultimately meaningless. How we prove our personal biases with "conclusive scientific proof" is what bears close consideration.

Many people are accustomed to reading newspaper or magazine articles that discuss scientific studies which point to or prove a conclusion. I have observed how people believe what they read without question, in part because most of us do not have the background necessary to dispute scientific findings, and in part because many of us believe that when scientific proof is demonstrated, all the scientists in the world are standing in white coats nodding their heads in approval. We naturally want to believe that scientific findings are met with unanimous consent, but in truth this is rarely so.

Scientific study is often like opening shutters in a darkened room. When the sun fills the room with light, we can conclude that the act of opening the shutters made the sun appear in the sky, or reason that the sun was already there and opening the shutters simply allowed the light to come through. Can you see how different conclusions can be drawn from the same evidence, and that we tend to interpret results based on what we are looking for.

## The Three Levels of Diet

Another important distinction that helps us understand the spectrumlike nature of nutrition is the three levels of diet: therapeutic, maintenance, and experimental. By distinguishing the proper use of each level of diet we can gain some insight into the confusion and disappointment that arise when a diet fails to meet our expectations, and we can consciously choose the level of diet on which we would like to work.

A therapeutic diet is a diet specifically intended to treat or heal a disease. Examples are juice or water fasts, diets to lower cholesterol or blood-pressure levels, and a long list of popular diets touted as curatives for a host of illnesses. Therapeutic diets often facilitate dramatic healing and are in widespread use in both traditional and alternative healing sciences.

Though therapeutic diets are successful in curing disease, this does not mean they will continue to work on an everyday basis once the body is healed. Often a diet provides therapeutic benefits for a specific period of time and loses its effectiveness when the natural limits of its healing powers are reached. We have seen an example of this in cleansing diets that have positive benefits yet cause negative reactions once the body moves into a building phase.

People often become confused at this point because they have seen the healing powers of the diet, yet witness its loss of effectiveness. They fail to recognize that like any medicine, a therapeutic diet is a specific medical intervention used for the duration of the disease. You would not continue to take aspirin even though your headache was gone, nor would you have your teeth drilled further once a cavity is filled.

A maintenance diet nourishes us in our sustaining phase—it is the staple fare used in everyday life, the business-as-usual diet. On this level of diet foods are chosen for their ability to nourish us for long stretches of time without harmful or imbalancing effects. The key to this diet is to remember that foods which successfully maintain the body now may be ill-suited at another time.

An experimental diet is the use of food as an evolutionary tool, a way to play with the possibilities of what a particular diet can do for the body. On an experimental diet we are the scientists of the body, asking questions such as, What would happen if I ate these particular foods? How would they affect my body, health, energy level, work output, and ability to think? Any foods that have unproven effects or that we have not used before present an opportunity to explore the unknown, to bring to our diet a sense of newness and discovery.

Taking vitamin supplements, for example, may be considered one way to use diet for experimental purposes. Proof enough exists of the *therapeutic* effects of vitamins and minerals—the use of supplements to treat disease conditions—however, the use of vitamins for maintenance purposes or for specialized life-style needs is a relatively recent phenomenon and largely experimental. By taking supplements we actively participate in human evolution, coaxing the body into greater (or lesser) levels of function.

Since the dawn of humankind the staple foods used to maintain the body have changed and evolved. Even now diet continues to change as we manufacture new foods, incorporate new growing methods, and change the way we live. Many people fail to see the evolving nature of diet and look at the diets of our distant ancestors to prove we were meant to eat a certain way, which is like excavating a tomb to prove we were meant to write on papyrus and drive chariots.

Whenever you read diet books or listen to nutritional advice, remember you are probably receiving information from those who are reading their own bodies and translating it onto yours, presenting their philosophy of life through beliefs about diet, and proving their biases through scientific conclusions that can be interpreted in other ways. Of course, we expect to find useful information when consulting expert sources, but the reality is that most authorities see only a small part of the nutritional spectrum, and no matter how much information we gather, we must inevitably make our own nutritional choices. Ultimately, the most reasonable view is this: Diet will vary from person to person, from one week to the next, and no matter what happens, nothing will stay the same for long.

### KEY LESSONS

- There is not one but a whole spectrum of nutritional systems suitable for human beings.

- For each person the appropriate diet depends on genetic predisposition, geography, cultural beliefs, personal preferences, and the dynamically changing needs of the body.

- People often believe that whatever diet worked for their body will work equally well for everyone else's.

- A nutritional philosophy is often part of a larger philosophy of life. When people passionately promote a diet, they are not just asking you to eat particular foods, they are asking you to espouse their view of the world.

- Nutrition experts often support their approach with scientific evidence that can be interpreted in several different ways.

- The three levels of diet—therapeutic, maintenance, and experimental—provide a key to understanding the results we can reasonably expect from a diet.

## REFLECTIONS

- Can you think of a time in your life when you believed in the superiority of a diet? Did the diet's effectiveness change? Any ideas why? Were there accompanying changes in your awareness?

- Can you recall examples of others around you promoting a particular diet? Did you feel as if you were being asked to embrace more than just a diet? Why were they so passionate about their diet? Was their approach effective? How did you respond? Have you ever experienced receiving nutritional advice that felt intuitively wrong for your body?

- Can you recall evidence of your body moving through cleansing, building, or sustaining phases? What do you eat during these different phases? How does your body feel? What do you experience on an emotional level?

- Have you ever been on a therapeutic diet? How did it benefit you? What were its limitations?

- Can you characterize your usual maintenance diet? What are your staples, the foods eaten most frequently? What is it about these foods that makes them work so consistently? Have your staple foods changed over the years?

- Do you ever use diet in an experimental fashion—either consuming foods not in your usual diet to see the results, or taking vitamin and supplement products? How do you go about experimenting with these foods? How do you measure the results?

- Exactly why do Chinese people eat differently from Italians? What can you tell about a culture from its cuisine?

- On the same day visit a supermarket, a health food store, an Oriental grocery, a bakery, a butcher shop, and a liquor store. Observe the people, the atmosphere, and the food. Then observe your reactions to each of these.

- Go to your local bookstore and browse through the following books: *Life Extension* (Pearson and Shaw), *Eat to Win* (Haas), *Food and Healing* (Colbin), and any books by Michio Kushi, M. F. K. Fisher, and Dr. Robert Atkins. What can you tell about their approach to food? Their approach to life?

# 4

# *You Eat What You Are*

Y ou have probably heard the popular phrase, You are
what you eat, a maxim implying that the body assumes
the characteristics of the food we ingest. Consume junk food
and a "junk body" results, or eat healthy food and a disease-
less body is formed. This saying is a clear distillation of the
scientific model of nutrition that considers the body to be the
sum of all the nutrients and chemical components of our
food.

Yet the statement, You are what you eat, tells only half the
story of nutrition. The other half is, You eat what you are.
That is, whatever we already are will determine the kinds of
foods we reach for and the body we will help create.

For instance, if you imagine yourself to have little willpower
or control in life, you will probably gravitate toward foods
that create the experience of lack of control in the body—
excess sweets, rich foods, or anything you consider "irresist-
ible." The more these foods are eaten, the more they are

desired and hence the belief, I have no willpower, is reinforced. On the other hand, if you imagine yourself to be well disciplined or even rigid, you will naturally reach for foods that maintain the experience of discipline in the body—bland foods, simple meals, and edibles that do not leave you craving for more.

Even nutritional deficiencies may be as much a product of how we think as it is an improper diet. For example, some of the symptoms of iron deficiency (anemia) include fatigue, weakness, lack of drive, and feelings of melancholy and helplessness. Do people with anemia suffer from this condition because the diet is low in iron-rich foods or because they are already melancholic in temperament and naturally reach for a low-iron diet that supports this condition? Similarly, are people with hypoglycemia (low blood sugar episodes) suffering from this condition because of excess sweets and a lack of high-protein and complex-carbohydrate foods in the diet or do they already have the attributes of the hypoglycemic temperament—mood swings and dramatic energy changes—and hence reach for a diet that perpetuates this state?

Of course there are no clear-cut answers to these questions, and certainly both perspectives contribute to our overall dietary patterns. The important point is that the scientific model—You are what you eat—holds the food solely responsible for creating the body, while the perspective, You eat what you are, shifts a portion of the responsibility back to us.

## Eating Our Attitude

Many of us are concerned about health and search for ways to prevent disease through diet and supplements, yet we often overlook the importance of an ingredient consumed at each meal—attitude. If you eat something "bad" for you with an attitude of guilt and self-punishment, the experience of the food will certainly be unnourishing—any toxins in the meal are made doubly potent simply by adding fear. Yet the same food eaten with an attitude of celebration may have a very different reaction in the body. Likewise, the healthiest foods may prove unhealthy if the motivation for eating them is based on a fear of disease rather than a love of life.

Years ago my father was diagnosed as having the highest-grade brain tumor possible and was given two months to live by his doctors, three if he underwent chemotherapy and radiation treatment. With this grim death sentence, he wisely explored alternative healing options, chose a macrobiotic diet, and for the next eight months followed this regimen to the letter. His determination was admirable, especially when considering how dramatic a shift this diet was from his usual fare.

At the beginning of the ninth month a brain scan revealed his cancer to be in complete remission. A once fatal tumor was gone without a trace. The doctors were speechless, my family was ecstatic, and yet my father was surprisingly low-key about his recovery. I could detect no discernible change in his attitude.

Several weeks later he was back in the hospital. He had suffered a mild heart attack. What seemed like a miraculous success story was suddenly a great mystery. How is it that the macrobiotic diet healed the most malignant brain tumor, yet could not prevent a mild heart attack? It was not until shortly before he died (four and a half years after his initial diagnosis) that I was struck with an insight into his condition.

My father never spoke about the seriousness of his condition nor did he face the possibility that he might die—sooner if not later. During the eight months on the macrobiotic diet he lived in terror of dying. His uncompromising dedication to the diet was, in fact, motivated by a fear of death rather than a love of life. On one level the diet had enough healing power to eradicate his tumor, yet it could not counteract the negative thoughts and feelings consumed with it that eventually weakened his heart.

## Food-Mood or Mood-Food?

Much has been written about the food-mood connection, the way that different foods affect our mood. Little attention, though, has been given to the mood-food connection, the manner in which our mood affects the digestion of food. Many of us have experienced the uncomfortable sensations in the body that occur when eating a meal during a stressful or hurried state—gas, cramps, intestinal pain, stomachaches, heartburn, and the feeling that food is just "sitting" in the stomach. During any kind of stress, whether a real or imagined one, the body clicks into the classic "fight or flight" response. This nervous-system mechanism is an evolutionary adaptation that protects us against outside dangers threatening biological survival—hostile attackers, natural disasters, and anything we must forcibly overcome or quickly avoid.

In the fight-or-flight response blood pressure increases, heart rate increases, blood flow is shunted away from the midsection and digestive system and toward the arms and legs, and digestive functions are shut down. All of the body's energies are rerouted for powerful arm and leg movements and heightened respiration used for fighting or fleeing. What is most intriguing about the fight-or-flight stress response is that during a stressful day at home or at work when there is no actual danger to your life, the body interprets the emotional stress as life-threatening, and the stress response clicks in to varying degrees, depending on the level of stress.

If you decide to eat a meal in this state, the blood flow to your digestive system may be as much as four times less than the usual amount, and nervous system impulses to the digestive system may have signaled a complete shut-down. You may be eating, but you will not be digesting. Depending on the intensity of the stress and the rate at which your digestive system returns to normal function, food may sit for hours in the stomach undigested or pass through the small intestines with nutrients only minimally assimilated. In addition, recent research has found that eating under stress reduces the amount of saliva in the mouth and the level of the enzyme amylase found in the saliva, which helps in the initial digestion of starches.

So no matter how healthy our diet, an unhealthy mood radically depreciates the nutritional value of a meal. We quite literally have less ability to digest food when our mind is improperly digesting life's experiences.

On the other hand, you may have noticed how a positive mood affects digestion. Whenever I ask people, "What is the best meal you ever had?" they often recall a meal that was notable not so much for the food, though it may have been superb, but for everything else they "ate" with the meal—the mood, the company, the ambiance, the room, the colors, and the conversation.

One woman recalled a visit to the Danbury Country Fair in Connecticut with a group of high-school girlfriends. They spent a glorious day together playing and exploring the fair, and as they were leaving they stopped at a food stand to buy pork chops for the long ride home. Though she usually felt sick whenever she ate pork chops and knew her digestive system could not handle them, she bought a jumbo bag like the rest of her friends rather than be excluded from all the fun.

As they drove down winding country roads the girl driving the car could not grip the steering wheel because her hands were covered with pork chop grease. The car swerved, and the girls laughed hysterically the whole ride home. Before she knew it, she had finished her entire bag of pork chops, and for some strange reason her body felt great—no queasiness and no heartburn. Her stomach was light and empty, yet she felt completely fulfilled and satisfied. It was the best meal she had ever had.

Weeks later, recalling her ecstatic pork chop experience, she purchased a bag to eat on her way home from school. No sooner had she finished than she was sick to her stomach. The pork chops felt nothing like the ones from the Danbury Country Fair, and she has not been able to eat pork chops since.

Another fascinating aspect of the mood-food connection is how deeper forms of nourishment like love and tenderness can apparently offset the harmful effects of a disease-forming diet. In one study scientists were testing a drug to lower cholesterol. The first stage in the study was to elevate the cholesterol level in test rabbits so the effectiveness of the drug could then be assessed. A large number of rabbits were placed on a high-cholesterol-forming diet, and their serum cholesterol levels were checked.

Quite unexpectedly one group of rabbits showed no increase in cholesterol level even though the drug had yet to be administered. Excited scientists looked to discover any unique genetic characteristics about this particular group of rabbits resistant to serum cholesterol increase, but no distinguishable features could be found. These rabbits were the same genetic strain, received the same food, and the same care as the rest. The scientists found only one difference with this special group of rabbits; the laboratory assistant in charge of those particular cages was an animal lover. Each day she would take the rabbits out of the cage, hold them, talk to them, and love them.

Although you will not find much scientific documentation on the nutritional value of love or the digestion-enhancing properties of laughter and celebration, can you see the implications of mood on food? And can you understand why nutrition goes far beyond the nutrient levels of a meal?

## The Nutrition of Relationship

The nutritional value of a meal is also given in the way the meal brings us into relationship with others. I recall the time when I returned home for Thanksgiving dinner during my first semester away at college. I had entered school a meat eater and was returning home a hard-core vegetarian. My family was excited to see me because I was the first of the children to make it to university level. They were eager to hear some words of higher education but unprepared for the surprise lecture I delivered at the dinner table.

As the turkey was served I discoursed at length on the evils of meat, speaking with authority about the poisonous effects of cholesterol, saturated animal fats, and hormone-injected turkeys. To my surprise the air of festivity I anticipated at the unveiling of these nutritional revelations was absent. People were silent, the mood was dreary, and no one seemed to be "getting it." What's more, my grandmother was heartbroken that I did not eat her turkey. It was the worst Thanksgiving I ever had.

The next decade of Thanksgivings followed a similar theme. My family felt I was a lost soul, and I believed they were living in the dark. Somehow, though, time changed my attitude toward food and toward life. One Thanksgiving I sat at the table and watched as my grandmother carved the turkey. I saw the love she poured into it and instantly knew that for her, eating the turkey meant I loved her—and not eating it meant I didn't. In that moment the choice for me was obvious. I wanted turkey.

Watching me eat was like seeing her grandson return from

the dead. The tension at the table melted away for the first time in years, the turkey felt great in my body, and the look of joy in my grandmother's eyes was worth eating all the turkey in the world.

When we say to someone, "Don't eat that food, it is bad for you," what they often hear is, "You are a bad person for eating that food." To have someone judge our choice of food or simply believe they are judging us is experienced as an affront to our fundamental right to existence. Tolerance and respect for the food preferences of others is a crucial ingredient of eating. Consuming "bad" food has never turned anyone into a bad person nor has eating "good" food made anyone a saint.

Despite its drawbacks, observing the food habits of others is a most popular way to "size people up." Have you ever noticed yourself assessing people by examining the food in their shopping carts or observed how people in a restaurant look at the food on a stranger's plate before they look at that person's face? Once I dined in a restaurant that featured a salad bar with a gargantuan selection of items and found myself intently observing the different combinations people put on their plates. Curiously, the man who sat down at the table next to mine had chosen precisely the same items as I had—tortellini, cucumber slices, alfalfa sprouts, one slice of tomato, and some bread sticks. The odds against this happening were astronomical, and I instantly felt a kinship with him and wanted to embrace him as if he were a long-lost brother. If he was eating the same foods I was, then surely he must be a wise and special man.

Eating similar food or sitting at the same meal is a ritual union. Whether it is a family barbecue, religious worshippers receiving the sacrament, or a bunch of guys drinking beer and watching a football game, eating joins us together. However different we may be in other ways, we are linked by a similar food contained within the body.

## The Subtleties of Nourishment

Of all the ingredients in a meal, the "subtle" ingredients are the least observable but often the most easily felt. Have you noticed how food that is "offered" by someone tastes different from food you prepare for yourself. For me, even a cucumber tastes different if someone else cuts, peels, and serves it with love. Just as food absorbs the flavor of spices, it absorbs the attitudes of those who cook and serve it.

Advertisers are keenly aware of the nutritional value of subtle ingredients like warmth, care, and familiarity. They market mass-produced foods that "taste just like Grandma used to make" or have that "real homemade flavor." Have you ever asked yourself exactly what it is that makes food taste homemade or what Grandma put in the pot to make the food distinctively hers?

Whatever our state of consciousness as we prepare a meal, that consciousness is absorbed by the food and is in turn what we become. Once I vacationed with a friend on Orcas Island in the Pacific Northwest. We volunteered to cook dinner for a week-long t'ai chi retreat at a beautiful resort in exchange for a beachfront cabin. The t'ai chi teacher dictated explicit instructions for the simple meal plan and its ingredients: rice and beans, steamed vegetables, and fresh bread with cheese and butter on the side.

Each evening we cooked with delight, mixing in the peacefulness and magic of our island experience. The t'ai chi group loved the food, and the teacher was equally pleased. They recognized the joy with which we served them and openly appreciated our efforts.

Dinner on the last evening proved to be a surprise, though. My friend and I argued over whose turn it was to do the laundry, could not reach an agreement, and carried our dissension into the kitchen, preserving a tense silence as we cooked. When the students finished eating the teacher walked into the kitchen and inquired what we had put into the food and why we had deviated from his instructions. He was disturbed because many of the students had stomachaches and the food tasted "off." We insisted it was the same quality ingredients used all week and that he should look elsewhere for the cause of the problem. But we knew the food was indeed contaminated, and its source was none other than our own discontent.

Even the way we offer food to *ourselves* affects our nutritional experience. One woman I know moved to Southern California to improve her health. She was suffering from severe allergies, food sensitivities, and chronic low immunity. She found a job in a vegetarian restaurant and worked three shifts a day to help pay her bills. In less than a year her health improved dramatically. She attributed it to the great weather and the three meals a day eaten at the restaurant, the healthiest food she had ever had.

Strangely enough, once her health improved and reached its peak, she slowly dropped back to her previous state even though her diet was unchanged and the weather was still warm. When she told me her story I was struck by one detail: She had not prepared a meal for herself in close to a year. In fact, her entire life-style for that time showed a strong deficiency in self-nourishing pursuits. She had little social life, took no time off from the restaurant, and had no creative outlets.

I suggested that her health might show improvement if she cooked just one meal for herself each day to bring to the restaurant and it did not matter what kind of food she cooked. To her, the idea sounded nonsensical especially since she was entitled to free meals at the restaurant. Still, she agreed, and much to her surprise she felt great again in several months' time.

As I saw it, to cook that one meal a day she needed to fix up her kitchen, plan a menu, shop for food, in short, to take time for herself. When food ceases to nourish, a deeper source of nourishment must be found. The original impetus to work in the restaurant and eat healthy food was a beautiful and timely self-nourishing act, yet she reverted to life on "automatic pilot" and lost touch with what truly nourished her in the first place. Cooking for herself meant nourishing herself on a deeper level. The food in the restaurant had the power to heal her, but it could not sustain her when self-love was absent.

Many people are caught in a similar bind of what I call the one-minute eater. For these people nourishment is secondary to taking care of business. Eating is no longer a basic need but a nuisance to be squeezed into the schedule. One-minute eaters are engaged in a fundamental battle—on one side stands their career or work obligations, and on the other is their need for nourishment and self-care.

Not only is nutrition a loser in this battle, but "nourishment" suffers as well. One-minute eaters have difficulty taking time to enjoy themselves, receiving nurturance from others, and listening to the promptings of their own hearts. If we cannot give the body what it needs, we are unlikely to have any success in caring for the soul.

I have counseled many Wall Street executives who were literally destroying themselves by overworking and maintaining poor health habits. Though they knew how their life-style affected them, their habits remained unchanged. Imagine some of the sharpest business minds in the world, experts prized by others for their superior management abilities, who cannot manage the fundamental necessities in their own lives. When our priority is personal success, it is often at the expense of our body's failure.

## Eating Our Roles

Perhaps the most important "course" consumed at any meal is the role we play and the lessons that role teaches us. At any given time in life we act out a particular part or personality. We may be in a rebellious role, a conservative mode, a money-making phase, a wandering period, a health-conscious stage, or a crisis time. Each part we play stays with us for a while, teaches us important lessons, then changes to whatever is next. And each role is associated with a particular way of eating.

Teenagers, for instance, often play a rebellious role—they constantly challenge old values and explore new ones. They act with regard to immediate gratification rather than future consequences. Telling teenagers what to eat is generally useless. They will choose whatever is most pleasurable and exciting, with little thought about its impact on their health (which is why I tell parents that the best nutritional advice to give teenagers is to find out what they want to eat and tell them to eat it). The teenager's diet is simply a reflection of their state of consciousness—they do not want rules, they just want options.

In my strict vegetarian days I played the role of disciplinarian not only with food but with people as well. I chose to avoid meat out of a deep respect for animals, yet ironically I had a disrespect for people who ate animals. Though I was rigid and self-righteous about many things in life during this phase, I did learn discipline and structure and saw the value of every act of nourishment. The food I chose to eat was simply a reflection of the way I chose to see life.

One woman I know had dreamed for many years of traveling the world but was afraid because her diet was so strict and would be impossible to maintain while traveling overseas. She felt as though she could not leave her hometown to fulfill her life's fantasy because her diet was limiting her. In truth, it was only her *thinking* about diet that was the limiting factor. She identified so strongly with her eating pattern that she felt obligated to conform to her diet rather than have the diet conform to her needs.

Eventually her dietary rules softened and the year-long trip around the world proved to be a wonderful opening in her life. She played the role of a traveler in many lands, opening up to new ideas and people, while sampling new ways of eating she had not thought possible for herself. It was no coincidence that her outward journey finally took place when her inner journey with diet deepened.

Each diet we follow is a reflection of the role we are playing at that particular time in life. We are never limited to a particular role or to the diet that accompanies it. The food we eat changes as we change. And by playing out each role wholeheartedly, while knowing somewhere inside that we are only acting out a part, we gracefully move from one phase of life to the next and gain a rare mastery seldom seen with eating.

## KEY LESSONS

- Nourishment is not limited to food alone. It includes all the ways we feed the many needs we have.

- Though the love, care, and consciousness we put into a meal cannot be measured, these are nevertheless real and crucial ingredients.

- Not only does food affect our mood, but mood affects the digestion of our food. Eating while in a stressful state decreases digestive capacity. Eating while in a positive emotional state increases digestive capacity.

- When we say to someone, "Do not eat that food, it is bad for you," what they often hear is, "You are a bad person for eating that food."

- When our priority is our career, it is often at the expense of the body. Effective time management in business means taking time to care for the needs of the body.

- The foods we eat often correspond to the particular role we are playing in life.

## REFLECTIONS

- In what ways does the statement, You are what you eat, apply to you? In what ways does the statement, You eat what you are, apply?

- Have you ever followed a diet out of fear? What were the results? How did you feel? Have you ever followed a diet out of a love for life? What was your experience of this diet? Can you pinpoint some of your reasons for following your present diet? Do these motivations and attitudes serve you?

- Have you experienced eating while under stress? What were the results? How did your body feel? Compare this to a celebrational eating experience. Was your digestion different?

- The next time you are in a state of reverence and awe for any reason, eat a meal and see if the taste is different.

- Are there times when you need to choose between what you want to eat for your health and what seems appropriate for a particular social event? Is the choice always clearcut? Are there times when it might be more nourishing to give up your dietary restrictions and enjoy what others are eating?

- How do you prioritize the care and management of your body? How much time is taken during the day simply to nourish yourself? Would more time benefit you? Your health?

- Have you noticed the "subtle ingredients" in meals prepared for you? What are the effects of these on the nutritional value of a meal?

- If you are the kind of person who does not cook for yourself, cook several meals in a day. See what happens.

- Cook someone else a meal with *feeling.* Observe the results. Did your friend eat more than the food?

# 5

# Good Food, Bad Food

M any of us, whether we are aware of it or not, have a laundry list of "good" foods and "bad" foods. Good foods are those that are believed to be healthy and somehow make you a better person if you eat them, and bad foods are believed to damage the body and make you a bad person if you eat them. What I suggest here, and what is perhaps one of the most crucial points of this book, is that *there is no such thing as a good food or a bad food.* I am not saying that different foods do not have either positive or negative effects on health. I am saying that no food is *morally* good or *morally* corrupt. For instance, when people say sugar is bad, there is often a hidden judgment that sugar itself is evil. Sugar may have negative effects on health, but I know of no candy bars that have ever conspired to rot people's teeth. Nor do I know of any food that comes with the *Good Housekeeping* seal of approval from God and his legions of angels. Food is neither good nor evil. It is neutral.

The value we ascribe to food depends on our preconceived notions and personal biases. Recall our previous example of the knife. Two people can look at a knife: An attack victim will see a weapon, and a cook something to cut vegetables with. Does this mean the knife itself is good or bad? The knife itself is neutral and can serve a number of functions.

This point is a subtle one yet most important, for whenever we label a food "bad," we immediately start to fear it, think about it, fight it, sometimes crave it, and in many cases label anyone who eats this bad food a bad person. Labeling chocolate as bad, for instance, sets up the internal dynamic that we must avoid it and protect ourselves from it. The more we consider it forbidden, the more we will think about it and desire it. And at least half of our craving is due to the fear of the chocolate. If we dropped our fear and dropped our belief that the chocolate was evil, the desire would be significantly reduced and in some cases eliminated.

Whenever we avoid anything, a homeostatic mechanism is set off driving us to reunite with it. This is a deeply programmed feature of the mind that cannot be averted. For example, if someone we love insults us and we feel hate inside, it would seem as if hating them would barricade them from our thoughts. Yet the hate only makes us think of them more, and though they may have insulted us only once, we replay it over and over in our mind, in effect repeating the original offense perhaps hundreds of times. Our thoughts will focus on that person until the issue is integrated, resolved, and made neutral. The same with food.

Many therapists treat certain food obsessions by telling their clients to eat as much of a "forbidden" food as they want, whenever they want, with absolutely no restrictions. People often react with shock to such a suggestion because on the one hand they believe this is "bad," and on the other hand they believe that "if I fully gave in to my desire, it would be insatiable. I would eat and eat and never stop." But extreme pleasure often turns into pain. For many people who fully allow themselves to binge on chocolate and enjoy it, the craving extinguishes itself. They either become physically sick or find that the pleasure simply wears off. The next time they eat chocolate the craving is radically diminished, and it is easier to experience satisfaction and let go of anxieties.

Since we view particular foods as bad, we consider our desire for those foods bad, which leads to seeing *ourselves* as bad for having the desire. And if in addition we give in to this desire, then we punish ourselves by feeling guilty, or we deprive ourselves of the desired foods for months.

Many people play a game I call Hide and Go Eat. Because they have labeled certain foods bad—sugar, ice cream, cake, et cetera—the act of eating them constitutes a crime. And, as any good criminal knows, the best way to commit a crime is to do it in secret. They hide doughnuts deep in the linen closet or conceal candy bars under the bedcovers and eat them when no one is around. In fact, people will conceal anything they have labeled bad in the hope that no one will discover their "criminal" nature. This includes sexual desire, desire for money and power, or any personal quality they feel ashamed of.

Often we may have no desire for a particular food but are attracted to it simply because it is forbidden or considered bad by others. When I was in the fifth grade a few of my friends discovered a candy none of us had known about. It was called Zotz. Zotz was a sucking candy that contained bicarbonate of soda and some unknown ingredients in the middle that on contact with the tongue would burst, pop, and fizzle like tiny firecrackers. This candy was an instant hit and became a sacrament among my small group of friends. We would suck on Zotz during class and giggle at each other when the edible fireworks commenced. Disturbed by the sounds of laughter and delight, the teacher finally caught on to our escapade and announced to the entire class that Zotz candy was forbidden in the classroom. The other children had never heard of Zotz candy before, but by the next day every kid had a package.

## How Moralizing Affects the Body

The implication of seeing food as morally good or evil runs even deeper, for when labeling food in this way, we instantly suppress the natural flow of biological information. We cut off the rich and complex messages that the body would otherwise feed back to us about the food we are eating. Let me explain this principle a little roundaboutly. Say, for instance, that a person you have never met walks into the room and I say to you, "Avoid that man. He is a bad person." Chances are, you will believe me. You will never get to know him, understand him, or experience his depth simply because of this initial judgment. The man might very well be a saint or a potential best friend, yet labeling him as bad has stopped your exploration process. The same is true with food.

If you conclude in your *mind* that chocolate is bad, you have not experienced this in the *body*. You have made a mental conclusion without the necessary physiological input. It's like deciding your bathwater is too cold without ever having put your finger in it. By coming to food without any preconceived moral judgments, we have an openness that allows for biological questioning and exploration. How does the chocolate affect my energy level? Does it hurt my teeth? Give me a headache? Do pimples appear on my face the next day? Do I feel drained an hour later? Does chocolate have positive effects on my body? Do certain brands of chocolate seem to be better for me than others? Is there any difference in how I feel when waking up in the morning after eating chocolate at night? Does a certain amount work well for me but anything more than that cause undesirable effects? Does it work well for me on some days but not on others?

By listening to body feedback and being open and attentive to the food we eat, we begin to make connections and draw conclusions between what we eat and how we feel. We discover pertinent information about our nutritional needs that no book could ever teach us. We may learn that certain foods yield a desirable effect in the body and others do not. If a food causes an undesirable reaction, all we need do is choose not to eat it. We need not label the food as bad or people who eat it as bad. A food that works well for one person may not do so for another. A food that agrees with us one day may not do so for another. We might even conclude that a food has an undesirable effect on our health, yet we like the taste so much that we choose to eat it occasionally. It is fine to eat something that we know is not best for the body as long as we make this choice *consciously*. Who is to say what is ultimately best for us to eat or not to eat in a given situation? I am not suggesting reckless eating. I am suggesting conscious eating—taking full responsibility for what you eat. Many people eat foods that affect their health negatively, and yet they are not aware of this or they choose not to be aware of it. As an old African saying goes, "Not to know is bad. Not to wish to know is worse."

Even when we label a food "good," a food that everyone might believe is beneficial to our health, we may still be stopping the biological feedback process. For example, if we believe that "sprouts are good for us" and eat them every day, we may well be eating more of our thoughts about the sprouts than the sprouts themselves. I have watched people force-feed themselves food they believed was good, yet they experienced little joy in the eating, nor do I imagine they were receiving the vibrant sensations that healthy food can provide. Food can be beneficial for health regardless of what we think, yet any time we eat with expectations about food that are born out of fear, the subtle energy of the body is suppressed. Eating sprouts out of fear quite literally silences signals and sensations in the body. In fact, whatever influences the mind—changing moods, personal beliefs, likes and dislikes, fears and insecurities, cultural and social conditioning—also influences the body. Health comes not only from eating good foods, but from thinking good thoughts and having a "healthy" attitude.

The payoff of categorizing food as good and bad is that it provides us with a sense of security. Nutrition is made into a set of cookbook formulas that eliminates any uncertainty and change. Of course, it is necessary in many cases to follow advice about what is good to eat and not so good to eat, particularly when we have little knowledge of nutrition and no understanding of how to discriminate between healthy and unhealthy foods. Yet this knowledge should serve as a foundation for the development of the body's intelligence and not its negation.

The challenge in seeing food as morally neutral is that we have to drop our long-held judgments and beliefs. We must admit that how we see things may not be entirely accurate, that the world is perhaps not as black and white as we thought. I recall a time while living in New York City when I believed I had released all rules about good and bad food. I was pleased that my diet was tension-free, and that I no longer judged people in terms of what they ate. But in my heart I knew there was one lone holdout—bacon. I was raised in a Jewish household where eating pork was forbidden, and though I could remember only a few of the Ten Commandments, I knew that one of them was, "Thou shalt not eat bacon." One day, during a particularly difficult time in my life—a relationship was ending, my apartment lease had expired, and my car had been towed from a no-parking zone—I was walking the streets in a daze, not really knowing where to go, when I noticed a sign in the window of a diner. It said, Bacon, Lettuce, and Tomato Special. I wandered in and without much thought ordered a bacon, lettuce, and tomato sandwich. And then another. And another. They were tasty and pleasantly fulfilling, but most amazingly, I felt a burden lifted off my shoulders. It made no sense, but I was giddy, deeply refreshed, and felt a freedom I had not experienced before.

Weeks later I made the connection between bacon and my life. So many of my most cherished beliefs about the world had been shattered, and the greatest pain of all was the realization that there was no certainty in my life, no set way to see things. My belief in the evils of bacon represented all this. It was one of my last long-cherished but useless beliefs about food. Eating the bacon sandwiches and enjoying them symbolically affirmed that there are no hard and fast rules in my life. The things I thought so terrible did not leave a bad taste after all. There was still hope for the world.

## KEY LESSONS

- There is no such thing as an intrinsically good or bad food. Food is neutral. We can assess the effects of food, though, as either desirable or undesirable.

- By labeling a food bad, we desire it and think about it more.

- By labeling food as bad, we suppress body wisdom—the natural information-gathering and feedback process that would otherwise inform us of the effects of food on our body.

## REFLECTIONS

- Make a list of the foods you consider good and those you consider bad. What makes these foods good or bad? Who says so? Can you think of anyone who would disagree with your findings? What arguments would they use?

- Have there been any foods in your life you once considered good but now consider bad, or vice versa? What brought about these changes? How did you back up your point of view then and how would you defend it now?

- As an experiment, for one week eat as much of the foods on your "bad" list as you like. Drop any ideas you have about how these foods will influence you. Observe their effects on your body as if you were a scientist.

- Eat a small amount of a food you consider *really* bad and never thought you would eat. How is your body affected? Your mind? Did something different happen from what you expected? What does this tell you about your relationship to food?

- Take a poll of your friends, family, and coworkers. Ask them which foods they consider good and which they consider bad. Compare the results. Why the differences? Can you tell how these labels affect their behavior? What can you learn about them by their assessments of good and bad foods?

- Compare the following magazines: *Vegetarian Times, Woman's Day, Sports Illustrated, East West Journal, Psychology Today, Prevention,* and *Field and Stream.* Who are the audiences for these magazines? Can you determine from their articles and advertisements the foods on their good and bad lists?

- Can you recall instances from your childhood when you were taught that certain foods were good or bad? Did you believe what you were told? Do you still believe it now?

# 6

## *The Quest for the Perfect Diet*

Because so many of us are accustomed to separating f
into categories of good and bad, a common result o
seen is "the quest for the perfect diet." People who search
the perfect diet believe that "if only I can find the one
way to eat, then I'll be forever healthy and happy."

By searching for the perfect diet we project onto our f
what we want from ourselves as people—perfection. We
tach to our diet the same impossibly high standards
rigorous rules we use to measure ourselves. Naturally we co
up "imperfect." The perfect diet contains the illusory prom
of perfect health. We relentlessly pursue such a diet beca
we believe, on some level, that it will make our body imm
tal. No longer will disease or death be feared. If by chance
do become sick or diseased, then we have not followed
diet correctly. It is we who are imperfect, not our thinki

By believing we can create a body that is changeless a
resistant to nature's forces, we mask our fear of dea

Though we have experienced sickness and see people all around us age and weaken, we somehow believe that "illness and death cannot touch me. My diet will make me immortal." We seek a healthy diet not out of love for the body, but from the fear it will grow old and die.

One of our strongest survival instincts is the urge to be at optimum health. This yearning is the underlying factor in the quest for the perfect diet. Yet we distort this instinctual longing and use the right intention, which is healthy eating, to lead us in the wrong direction—perfect eating. We take a biological drive that says, "I must eat in the best way possible because a balanced diet is essential for health," and twist it into, "I must eat a perfect diet because it will make me perfect. If I do not, I am imperfect and therefore unworthy as a human being."

Many people who believe they have found the perfect diet profess that their way of eating is the ultimate panacea and anyone not subscribing to their diet is unaware of the "real truth." Perfect dieters often discuss their way of thinking and eating in much the same way as religious fundamentalists air their doctrines. They emphasize that their diet works not only for the body but for all aspects of life. It cleanses toxins, heals ailments, and enlightens ignorant minds. Life is made easy because we no longer need to concern ourselves with the fluctuating needs of the body or make the nutritional adjustments that a constantly changing life demands.

Those who search for the perfect diet often subscribe to different vegetarian, macrobiotic, and raw-food-diet approaches. Research and experience have proven these ways of eating to be effective in promoting health and healing disease, but the false hope of perfection leads to an endless cycle of struggles and disappointments. Each of these systems has well-defined rules about what and how to eat. To the outsider these rules seem difficult to follow, and indeed, even for the

insider, they are. People work intensively at following such a diet and become completely absorbed in it. They spend much of their waking day thinking about perfection through food, eating it, and explaining why it was so good to eat. Enthusiasts are literally "consumed" by their diet.

Their devotion increases when they experience an initial phase of health benefits—proof indeed that they are on the right path. However, the promise of eternal health and happiness is never fulfilled. People become discouraged and stray from the diet. A vegetarian may commit a sin and eat meat, a raw-foodist may eat something cooked, or a macrobiotic might indulge in a hot fudge sundae.

By breaking the rules perfect dieters experience a sense of temporary relief. Because they have built up so much tension following their diet, forbidden foods provide them with immense pleasure. They are given a glimpse of freedom from their self-imposed prison. And yet by giving in to a craving, perfect dieters become guilt-ridden and seek atonement by promising to follow the diet more perfectly than before, which makes life even more difficult.

Ironically, any benefits of the diet are often outweighed by the tension and anxiety built up in maintaining it. The guilt experienced when eating forbidden food creates more toxins in the system than the actual food. Furthermore, the tension caused by resisting forbidden food can be equally toxic.

Another concealed trap in the quest for the perfect diet is moral judgment. Perfectionism and judgmentalism walk hand in hand. People often act as if they are on a crusade, and anyone not sharing the same mission is morally inferior. Because perfect eaters judge themselves, they naturally judge others. "If I am bad for not following my diet perfectly, then you must be *really* bad for not following it at all!"

Consequently, they become socially isolated, fearing group situations where perfect food is not on the menu. Instead of using food to celebrate life and share with others, eating becomes a source of alienation. "If you don't *eat* like me, you obviously don't *think* like me, and therefore you aren't worth associating with."

Friends and relatives of perfect eaters are often frustrated since they do not understand the strange diet nor the intense devotion. In extreme cases, perfect dieters exile themselves from friends and loved ones. The severity of their rules shuts out deeper forms of nourishment—sharing, celebration, and love. Of course the quest for the perfect diet is born out of a sincere desire to nourish oneself fully and attain a high level of health and personal satisfaction. Ultimately, however, it is the acceptance of imperfection that opens the doorway to the happiness that perfect dieters seek.

One young woman at a lecture I presented was eager for specific, hard-line information about what to eat and what not to eat. As she told the group about the years she had spent searching for the best diet, her tone of voice grew desperate. She was frustrated and confused because none of the diets had worked the way she wanted them to. I suggested to her that there is more to our relationship with food than finding the right way to eat, and that when searching for the perfect diet we are perhaps harboring a secret fear or making an unrealistic promise to ourselves. She burst into tears as she began to understand that she had been promising herself that if she found the perfect way to eat, she would not die of cancer like her mother. For many agonizing months she had watched her mother deteriorate and felt deeply abandoned when she finally died. Images of her mother's disease-ridden body had haunted her, and diet became a false hope of health and immortality. In this way, she avoided grieving for her mother and had never faced the inevitability of her own death.

In a letter she sent sometime later, she observed:

*I never suspected there was something more
than food as my issue, but during the work-
shop it just clicked about my mother's
deterioration and death from cancer of
the bowel . . . I learned that I am more
than my body, and that somehow I
will live on with my own children as
my mother now lives on in me. I see now
how I needn't be an absolute perfectionist,
and that I can let go into uncertainty. By
accepting that I will fall ill sometimes
regardless of diet, yoga, or exercise, I
live more in a place of trust with life
and death. These are my new guidelines in
anything I do—relax, be moderate, and
trust.*

## The Promise of High-Tech Nutrition

Another way we search for the perfect diet is by placing
unrealistic expectations in the powers of science and technology. We count on them to unlock all secrets of the universe
and solve the problems of life. We believe science will provide
us with supplements and high-tech food that stamp out disease and maximize brain power and sex appeal. By viewing
the universe as if it were one big complicated machine, we
inevitably view the body as if it were a machine. We exercise
it, jog it, test it, and analyze it. We do not see the body as a
whole, dynamic, integrated organism but as isolated parts. We
consume B-vitamins for the nervous system, vitamin E for the
cardiovascular system, amino acids for the musculoskeletal
system, and even suntan pills for the "tanning system." We
appear to be nourishing the body scientifically, but in reality
we are not so much caring for the body as we are doing things

*to* it. The body becomes a robot, commandeered by the mind's concept of how a body should function.

By relying *solely* on outside information about the body—from books, doctors, and other experts—we are alienated from our innate body intelligence. The richness, emotion, sensitivity, drama, and uncertainty that make the body "human" are forgotten. What is left is a shell that runs on nutrients. Thus, we view food merely as a collection of chemicals: milk for calcium, brussels sprouts for anticancer nutrients, bread for fiber, and oranges as a convenient package for vitamin C. We no longer consider how our food was prepared, who prepared it, how it feels, where it was grown, or even *if* it was grown. Eating is not a festive and sensuous experience, nor is nourishment symbolic of love, connectedness, nurturance, and fulfillment. Rather, nourishment is reduced to "nutrition"—vitamins, minerals, proteins, carbohydrates, and facts—just the hard, cold facts.

Of course, there are important benefits to reducing food to its basic elements. Unlocking the secrets of the molecular nature of food has given rise to the science of nutrition and to important discoveries in our knowledge of health and medicine. Problems arise, however, when we *oversimplify* food. By reducing food to its chemical components alone, we lose the nuances of eating. It is no different from discussing a great Rembrandt by analyzing the pigments in the paint.

Advertisers are quick to capitalize on dreams of technological perfection by offering "the most complete nutritional system," "everything your body needs," and "the formula for ultimate performance." They sell and we buy imagined nutritional perfection.

One man I know visited a nutrition-oriented medical doctor who prescribed a number of supplements to help heal his chronic allergies. Though he was highly skeptical of this approach, the regimen worked and consequently he became a convert to supplements and started poring through all the literature in the field. He began to use supplements to eliminate his "tired spells" and provide him with a source of sustained energy. For over a year he took, by his own estimates, about sixty-five different kinds of vitamins, herbals, enzymes, amino acids, and miscellaneous products. Sometimes he took as many as twenty different supplements per day.

When I first met him he had not yet experienced any significant improvements but felt confident that with the right combination of supplements, success was just around the corner. I suspected his motivation for taking so many supplements—namely his fear of not living up to some imagined standard of perfect health—was the force draining his energies. His anxieties were taking their toll in tired spells.

I advised that before we proceeded with a new strategy, he should eliminate all supplements for two months so that we could assess his condition. His heart almost stopped. It was as if I had asked him to walk off a cliff. After a while he courageously agreed. In two months I called him and we chatted over the phone. I asked if he was ready to discuss his tired spells and optimum energy supplement plan. Surprisingly, he replied that supplements were no longer so important to him as before. He was sick of taking so many pills and trying to figure out why he was so tired. He was experiencing newfound energy and was liberated from the disease that drained him—fear.

Many people interested in losing weight place similar unrealistic expectations in technology by believing that some day soon science will discover a new pill that will make us thin. We'll be able to eat all we want without getting fat. Science will even manufacture synthetic fats and sugars that have no calories so we can enjoy all our favorite foods without guilt. Whether or not technology can provide these innovations without hidden side effects that harm the body is debatable. The important point, however, is this: By holding false promises about what may or may not happen in the future, we stop ourselves from changing *now.* Rather than engage in the process of transforming our habits, a process capable of producing the lasting change we seek, we often choose to live with the fantasy of a quick-fix solution through technology.

## The Cellular Dynamics of Nutrition

The quest for perfect nutrition teaches us an important lesson: Nourishment is not *just* "nutrition." Nourishment is the nutrients in the food, the taste, the aroma, the ambiance of the room, the conversation at the table, the love and inspiration in the cooking, and the joy of the entire eating experience.

Even at the cellular level, nourishment is not derived exclusively from nutrients in food. Nourishment comes from the *process* our body undergoes to digest and assimilate those nutrients. Many of us believe that only vitamins, minerals, proteins, carbohydrates, and fats—the end products of digestion—are what nourishes. But equally important is the work the body must do to extract the nutrients from food and utilize them properly. In other words, nutrition is how the body processes food. It is the physical and chemical challenge the body faces in the breakdown of food in the mouth, the churning and the enzymatic digestion in the stomach, the absorptive process in the intestinal villi—the whole range of digestive activities. The process of digestion *is* nutrition.

The digestion of food is analogous to the lifting of weights. A weight lifter doesn't build muscle because two hundred pounds of weights are in his hands. It is not the weights that build muscle, but the process the body must go through—the weight lifting—that does it. Likewise, it is not just the nutrients in food that nourish, but the entire process the body undergoes to extract and assimilate those nutrients. It is as if the digestive system were one big muscle, and food the weight it must lift. With this in mind, the drawbacks of putting our nutritional emphasis exclusively on supplements are obvious. Why swallow large amounts of pills when the body is ideally nourished through the process of *extracting* nutrients from the food?

Scientists have long known that a diet of pure chemical nutrients cannot sustain human life. No matter what combination of substances is used, pure nutrients simply cannot replace real food. In one study, scientists at NASA were looking for the most simple, compact, and ideal diet for astronauts in space. Test subjects were fed all the daily required nutrients in chemical form. They consumed vitamins, minerals, protein, carbohydrates, fats, and fiber mixed with water. They received no food in the diet—no meat and potatoes for dinner and no cream pie for dessert—just the recognized isolated nutrients that comprise those foods. On this diet test subjects suffered from immune dysfunctions, bone loss, digestive disorders, internal bleeding, and impaired mental functioning, to name just a few symptoms. Because they had no food to exercise the full range of muscular, enzymatic, and hormonal components of digestion, subjects were left only partially nourished.

The problem we face then is not science, nutrition, or supplementation. The problem is the belief that we can overcome disease and death with technology. Supplements are meant to augment food, not replace it. Science is meant to teach us about our world, not remove us from it. And food is meant to nourish us, not merely provide nutrients.

## KEY LESSONS

- We often have the same unrealistic expectation about diet as we do about ourselves—perfection.

- The anxiety produced in maintaining a perfect diet can be more damaging to the body than any imperfect foods we may eat.

- By waiting for technology to save us, we prevent ourselves from changing now.

- By removing nourishment from nutrition, we lose the qualitative aspects of food such as love, nurturance, fulfillment, and celebration and replace them with quantitative aspects such as nutrient content and calories.

- Nutrition doesn't come from nutrients alone. It comes from the *process* our body undergoes in digesting and assimilating those nutrients.

## REFLECTIONS

- How do the standards you set for your diet relate to the standards you set for yourself as a person? Are these standards realistic?

- How do you judge yourself when you don't follow your diet? How does this judgment affect you?

- What do you honestly expect your diet to do for you? Are these expectations practical? Do you know anyone who has achieved these expectations on this diet? How can you look at your diet more realistically?

- What role do nutrition and scientific knowledge of eating play in your life? Would it benefit you to focus on nutritional understanding more? Less?

- If you are a meat eater, imagine for a moment that you are a radical vegetarian. How do you see the world? What convincing argument for vegetarianism would you give to a meat eater?

- If you are a vegetarian, imagine yourself to be a hard-core meat-and-potatoes person. Argue your case for a meat diet to a vegetarian. See the world through a meat eater's eyes.

- Go to a restaurant you normally wouldn't visit—vegetarian, Japanese, Indian, McDonald's, Dunkin' Donuts, or a roadside diner. Act as if you eat there every day. Order something, eat it, and note your general impressions and experience.

- Go to a university library and read through any scientific nutrition textbook. Learn as much as you can. Then read through Kim Chernin's books on eating disorders, *The Obsession* and *The Hungry Self*. Compare your learning experiences from each.

- Imagine you are a big businessman and have the opportunity to make millions of dollars simply by marketing a new weight-loss product. How do you feel about yourself? What are your most important concerns in this undertaking? Now imagine you are an overweight person and would like to purchase a weight-loss product. How do you feel about yourself? What are your main concerns in purchasing a product?

# 7

# The Eater's Mind

Have you ever noticed that one of the most fundamental myths of western civilization—the tale of Adam and Eve—is based upon the act of eating something forbidden? In this cryptic story Adam and Eve dwell in the idyllic Eden wanting nothing and living as children in bliss. God explains to them that they have everything they need and can do as they please except for one thing: They may not eat fruit from the tree of knowledge. As the tale unfolds, first Eve, and then Adam, is tempted to eat the fruit. They do and immediately they feel guilty, embarrassed about their bodies, and fearful of God, who now casts them out of the garden to fend for themselves.

Like any great allegory, there are many levels of interpretations to the Eden myth. In our interpretation the story symbolizes the initial journeying forth of human beings into conscious awareness. The Garden of Eden symbolizes the unconscious bliss of the child. The fruit of the tree of knowledge symbolizes the point of separation, the knowledge that we are a unique and separate self. By eating the fruit, Adam and Eve feel "different" from God, no longer merged in the paradise of childhood where wild animals are tame, where all our needs are fulfilled, and where it seems as though we will live forever.

Because they realize their separateness, they feel naked and ashamed of their bodies, the very basis of selfhood and existence. When we feel apart from the Divine, we inevitably are alienated from the body. Though their plight may seem an unfortunate one, Adam and Eve were not tempted to do something bad. They were tempted into consciousness. The serpent represents not some outside evil force, but the primal evolutionary impulse within each of us that lures us into awareness, literally tricking us into participation in life so we may fully experience both the imperfection of our humanity and the awesomeness of our divinity. There was no other way because the unfolding of self into higher states of knowing *is* the natural order of human development.

As we well know, whenever someone warns us not to touch a tantalizing delicacy in the refrigerator, we are already making plans to eat it the moment that person is gone. What Adam and Eve were told was this: "Do not believe you need to go outside yourselves to attain true knowledge. Do not believe you need be anything more than you already are. Do not believe you are separate from divinity." As we have seen, though, whenever something is stamped "forbidden" or labeled "wrong," we naturally seek to integrate it. This is an inherent function of the mind, to resolve the existence of opposites—good and evil, pleasure and pain, life and death. Adam and Eve needed to gain a knowledge of their separateness, to experience the nakedness, aloneness, and harshness of earthly life, for, indeed, no one can make life's journey untouched.

Each of us re-creates the Eden story in our own life. We grow out of the unconscious wholeness of the small child into self-awareness. We leave the blissful ignorance of the garden of childhood so that we may return to our prior connectedness to the spiritual source with a newfound awareness.

## The Spiritual Source

As we have seen, according to the perennial philosophy all beings arise from a spiritual source. This is the realm of experience where we feel an interconnectedness with all creation, a fundamental acceptance of our existence and the circumstances of life, and a heightened state of sensation and perception that draws us into our fullest participation with the world.

Tiny infants exist in a state that closely resembles the enlightened awareness that comes from a connectedness to the spiritual source. An infant is "one" with its surroundings, experiences the world as new in each moment, has a natural excitement for life, and strives to become nothing more than what it already is. And yet the child is not in a truly enlightened state because of the lack of a sense of "I," no experience of itself as a separate entity. A baby experiences no differences between itself and a rattle, its hand and someone else's hand. All is "one" because everything is experienced as a primordial undifferentiated oneness. The child is in bliss but the bliss is "prepersonal."

Gradually the infant learns that it is distinct from its rattle, and develops a sense of "I." But rather than emerge as a distinct self that is part of the spiritual source, the baby emerges as separate from it, for during the early years of life, when the child develops a sense of uniqueness, it is also learning that life is painful. It experiences the anxiety of separation when the mother leaves, the physical tension of not receiving instant gratification whenever it wants something—love, touch, or food; the pain of living in a body that undergoes sickness, coughing, stomach cramps, and high temperatures; the confusion of absorbing the complex values of an adult world—toilet training, "good" behavior, "correct" eating habits; and an endless number of expectations and rules from the world around it.

Consequently the child adopts the belief that "I am not enough as I am." It learns that it is a unique self, but it feels severed from its previous wholeness and experiences a growing sense of aloneness and insecurity. The rest of life is spent in search for wholeness, the continued attempt to heal the wounds of separation.

## Ego and Fear

Psychologists and philosophers have noted that the sense of "I" we call the ego is what distinguishes the human being from the rest of the animal kingdom. If a bear attacks someone, it is not required to stand trial, defend itself, or spend time in prison. No one cross-examines it to assess its true motive for attacking because the bear has no unique sense of self. It is bound by the laws of nature, and acts upon "bear instincts." When a human being attacks, he or she is accountable because each of us, on some level, understands the concept of "I" and the sacredness of life. We realize the importance of other lives because we know the importance of our own.

The ego as we are defining it here is not something negative. Quite the contrary, its development is a fundamental step in human unfolding. But because we adopt the core belief that "I am not enough as I am," the ego's original function of the maintenance of a unique identity connected to the spiritual source is distorted into the maintenance of a unique identity that is separate from it. And from this condition fear arises.

Our primal sense of fear can profoundly influence the way we live our lives—the goals we strive for, the people we surround ourselves with, the thoughts we think, and the decisions we make. Fear, like all emotions, follows thought. In other words, because the ego holds the thought "I am not good enough," fear arises. If someone compliments you on your new hairstyle, you may think, "This person is very sweet and sincere," and hence the emotion that follows will be happiness. If you think, "This person is insincere and trying to smooth-talk me," you may respond with feelings of anger. First comes the thought, then comes the emotion. To an ego that holds the thought "I am separate and alone," fear naturally follows, and this fear will drive us to act in ways that reduce the anxiety fear creates.

The catch is that fear distorts our perception. When acting from fear, we see what isn't there and don't see what is there. If we fear speaking in front of a group, for example, we may imagine that people are judging us harshly or secretly laughing at us, while in reality they may be amazed at our courage and enjoying our words. Fear has distorted our perception. If we cling to someone out of fear of losing them, we may blind ourselves to their faults or pretend they possess qualities that they do not. Because fear distorts the ego's perceptions, its strategies become paradoxical. On the one hand, the ego tries to maintain a healthy sense of self-identity and bring us into a fulfilling relationship with the world. On the other hand, the ego works to defend its sense of unworthiness because it believes that its separateness and the fear that results *are* its source of power and fulfillment.

This confused thinking is funneled into our relationship to food, from which results an endless assortment of paradoxical eating behaviors. For example, many people decide to eliminate a certain food from their diet overnight—sugar, coffee, dessert. They have probably chosen an impossible goal because this food is deeply ingrained in their diet and is perhaps an addiction. Going "cold turkey" would put them through intense physical or psychological withdrawal and is simply too difficult a path for their personality type. They attempt it anyway, fail, and lament their lack of willpower, secretly proving their core belief that "I am no good." One woman I know promised herself to lose thirty-five pounds in four months—in time to look her best for a wedding attended by friends she had not seen in years. She did not want to feel humiliated in front of her old college crowd because she had grown plump. She admitted to me from the outset that she was not feeling up to a diet, did not want to exercise, and knew she could not lose the weight, yet she had to give it a try. She dieted, failed, felt depressed, and as punishment for her "weakness" chose to stay home from the wedding she so dearly wanted to attend. The only weakness was in her thinking—setting herself a goal she knew could not be achieved.

Fear also drives us to create imaginary problems that we earnestly try to solve. For example, we may hold the belief that "I am unlovable by men" or "I am unlovable by women." Now, we honestly have no way of knowing that all men or all women do not love us, and the chances are that this is an inaccurate conclusion, yet we are capable of making such sweeping generalizations and living them out. Some people create the imaginary problem that "My health is not perfect" (whose health *is* perfect?) and use methods and medications that cause real illness, while others may have the imaginary problem that "My life is not going as it should" (how *should* life actually go?) and turn to overeating or bingeing, which produce real problems. Can you see how fear distorts our perceptions?

Perhaps the most common behavior born out of fear is the

search for immediate solutions, quick-fix methods to alleviate anxiety but provide only temporary relief. Because lasting solutions require self-reflection, sincere effort, and time, we often grow impatient and want change now. We turn to whatever will help us forget the pain we experience in the moment. Anything we do can function as temporary relief— sports, exercise, work, relationships, movies, sleep, or eating. Of course, nothing is inherently wrong with any of these; it is simply a matter of how we use them. We all need sleep, but how many of us fall into bed when feeling lonely, depressed, or unwilling to face the world? And everyone needs food, but how many of us use eating when the hunger we have cannot be satisfied by food?

## Symbolic Substitutes

By now you are probably aware of this fundamental paradox in human nature: A part of us wants inner peace and transcendence, and another part of us actively fights against it. Each of us instinctively intuits our prior wholeness, the spiritual source that lies hidden within. We are born with an evolutionary impulse that drives us toward the fulfillment of our greatest potential. If you have ever felt a "calling," an inner urge to be something more, it is the evolutionary impulse sparking you toward unfoldment. This drive is as real and as demanding as the inborn drive to eat, drink, or procreate. At the same time, however, the ego seeks to maintain its condition of separateness and aloneness. It fears its own annihilation because true fulfillment entails the healing of our separation, the integration of the ego into its original function—the healthy maintenance of our unique sense of "I."

Because of this basic dichotomy, we seek transcendence in ways that actually prevent it. When we desire something too difficult to attain, we reach for the closest approximation, a symbolic substitute. If we lack personal power, we may seek money and influence as a substitute for this quality. If we lack stability and roots, we may build a lavish home to overcome our sense of insecurity. If we feel a lack of meaning or excitement in life, we may turn to food as the best available substitute. It is a brilliant strategy of the mind to reach for substitutes when we cannot acquire what we really want. Why not reach for food when we are feeling lonely, or search through the refrigerator when life is a little dull? Substitutes can serve a useful purpose in our day-to-day existence. Yet they work against us when we hold to them exclusively as a means for true fulfillment.

Symbolic substitutes are often experienced as intense desires. A desire is defined here as something we believe we *must* have for peace of mind; for example, we may desire particular people, possessions, or experiences. Desires are born out of the belief that only something "outside" can complete us. In other words, the ego projects our innate sense of wholeness outward. It says, "If I am unwhole and separated, then my missing pieces must be somewhere out there." So we embark on a mission to recapture our missing pieces in other people, places, possessions, anything that gives us the temporary experience of wholeness.

The desire for a symbolic substitute carries a hidden promise. If we desire fame, the hidden promise might be "When I am famous, then people will admire and accept me." Or if we desire an ideal body, it might be "When I am thin, people will love me and my life will truly begin." These hopes and promises are seldom in our conscious awareness. However, they reveal themselves once we achieve what we desire. So for the people who finally do become famous, they may feel even more alone and misunderstood, and for the people who do lose weight, they may find themselves to be no more happy or in love with life. Just thinner.

Symbolic substitutes do provide temporary relief from our fears, but because these fears are imaginary to begin with, the desires we fulfill are imaginary and the real need is never satisfied. And this is why the ego is unwilling to let go of its intense need for substitutes. The letting go of a substitute immediately reveals its illusory nature and unearths the pain of our attachment. For example, when we let go of our attachment to coffee, alcohol, tobacco, or sugar, we often go through withdrawal symptoms, painful physical manifestations of the emotional suffering we experience inside. The relief we believed we were receiving reveals itself only as a shadow, and the pain lying beneath is finally exposed. These withdrawal symptoms must make their way through the body to release the biological craving. This allows the heart to experience the pain it secretly held and to let go of it once and for all. Interestingly, these same principles also apply to psychological "attachments." We quite literally go through withdrawal symptoms when leaving relationships, grieving over the death of a loved one, being rejected at school or work, or letting go of any fantasy that has proved unattainable.

Symbolic substitutes we believe we must have and use repeatedly are called attachments. Extreme attachments, particularly where the body becomes "attached" to a substitute and must have it, are called "addictions." Ultimately, all addictions are substitutes for the spiritual source.

Substitutes can provide us with either some temporary relief or a long-term painful addiction. Food in particular is one of our most faithful substitutes. It warrants special consideration because it functions as a stand-in for something human beings seem to seek most—love.

## Food and Love

From our earliest moments in life food and love are inseparably linked, forming a union that remains faithful and un-
broken. Held in its mother's arms the newborn not only
receives good nutrition as it suckles but is completely nourished. It is being touched, loved, sung to, spoken to, and
cared for in a way that is experienced only once in a lifetime.
And because a newborn does not separate these different
sensations, because things and events are not yet distinct at
this early age, food is love and love is food.

All eating is archetypically linked with this early memory
of food and love as a unified experience. When we think of
food we see love, nurturance, and the womb of the world.
Most of us have been upset about something, eaten, and then
felt better. Indeed, both the Yiddish and Italians have an old
saying, "There's no problem a little food wouldn't solve." No
matter how miserable life may be, food helps us temporarily
forget. Like the hypnotic effect of a campfire or the soothing
sound of a waterfall, eating draws us out of the mind's turmoil
and into the primal somatic experience of self-nourishment.
As the psychologist Bernd Jager says, "Food always offers us
a base, a ground for our existence."

One woman I counseled told me how much she loved food
and how it brought her such immense satisfaction. She would
sing the praises of cheesecake, brownies, and all her favorite
desserts and provide detailed information about the best
places to find the most delicious and esoteric sweets. She
seemed to be in love with food and deriving continuous
satisfaction from eating. Yet as I learned more about her, she
revealed her deep dissatisfaction with her marriage, appearance, and lack of meaning in life. She did not really "love"
food; she loved the way eating provided a temporary escape
from her troubled world. She was not so much in an experi-

ence of love as she was addicted to eating's narcotic effect.

When we say, "I love to eat double-dipped chocolate ice cream cones," what we often mean is, "I love the way eating certain foods takes my mind off personal problems. I like the temporary high I receive from eating." Most of us have successfully used eating as a momentary source of "instant love." Of course, food *is* a faithful source for love, and certainly there is nothing wrong with turning to food for an extra boost. It becomes problematic, though, when "loving food" takes the place of "loving life."

Can you imagine what life would be like if we loved ourselves as much as we love food? If we looked forward to the pleasure of our own company as much as we look forward to dinner? Loving oneself is as natural as feeding oneself. In fact, if we truly loved food, on a deeper level we would be experiencing love for ourselves. When the heart is happy, the simplest foods bring immeasurable delight. But when the heart turns against itself, even the best of foods fail to satisfy.

Food alone will never make us happy. If it could bring lasting happiness, it would have done so long ago. If you are not convinced of this, just think of a time when one of your favorite foods made you happy and satisfied. Now recall the other moments when the same food did not produce this result. Why isn't food consistent? Why does it bring happiness one moment, but not the next?

The answer is simply this: The food hasn't changed at all; we have. Our experience of food is really an experience of ourselves. On many occasions I have commented to my host or dinner companion that "this is the best meal I have ever had," and though I have said this perhaps hundreds of times, I've meant it every time. In each instance I felt fulfilled with myself and completely satisfied with my company. I was fully absorbed in the moment with no desire to do anything other than sit, eat, and enjoy. Yes, the food was good, but secondary to everything else. The food could not be better because *I* could not be better.

## Seeing Through the Mouth

To the metaphoric mind, food not only appears as love, but may assume many forms depending upon who is looking. To a woman concerned with maintaining a slender body, food may appear as fat. To a man concerned with building his body, food means muscle. To a scientist interested in the study of nutrition, food represents a collection of chemicals. Or to someone concerned with healing a disease through diet, food can be medicine. Perhaps the most primary metaphor through which we view food *and* the world is that of nourishment. Human beings continually search for whatever nourishes, that which tastes good, feels good, or looks good. Nourishment is anything that sustains us, that gives us the feeling of being "more."

Biologically, nourishment is encoded in our genes as the body's longing for perpetuation of itself through food and procreation. Psychologically, nourishment is encoded as our longing for perpetuation through creativity, relationship, community, work, and the exchange of ideas. Spiritually, nourishment is encoded as our longing for self-realization. Whether it is a warm meal, a warm fire, a warm friend, or a warm feeling, the metaphoric mind interprets each as nourishment and will substitute food whenever other sources of nourishment run low.

Indeed, the newborn child does not see the world primarily through its eyes—it sees through the mouth. Biological survival and orality are inseparably linked. From our earliest moments we reach for that which nourishes us—the breast. This instinctive grasping for nourishment through the mouth is so important to survival and so well encoded in the nervous system that even as adults we continue to search for nourishment through oral gratification—smoking cigarettes, chewing gum, sucking candies, "munching," "pigging out," nail-biting, pencil-chewing, and a long and interesting list of others.

Have you noticed how children explore things by tasting them? Whatever they can grasp is put into the mouth to assess its qualities and its essence. The mouth is our original organ of perception, the conduit through which we incorporate the world. As Freud and others have shown, "The oldest and truest language is that of the mouth: the oral base of the ego." This is as true for the "primitive" people of our culture—children—as it is for primitive cultures throughout the globe. As the historian Erich Neumann has shown, the initial creation myths of virtually all primitive cultures as well as for the Greeks, Romans, Chinese, Africans, and Indo-Europeans center around somebody eating someone or something else— Adam and Eve eat an apple, Shiva swallows up the oceans, the Egyptian goddess Nut gives birth to the sun in the east and swallows it in the west. These cultures saw through the perspective of the mouth because from the earliest stages of human history, food and hunger were the primary movers. Life revolved around finding food, killing it, cooking it, and eating it.

Since the first protolife forms appeared in the primal oceanic soup, the world has been eating itself—plants eat the soil, animals the plants, people the plants and the animals, and the earth finally eats the remains of all the life it has sustained. Nothing can escape eating and nothing can escape being eaten.

This principle applies not only to the biological realm but to the psychological as well. We may say to someone, "I love you so much I could eat you," or we can fear someone so much that we are afraid of "being eaten alive." We are continually "consuming" new ideas or feeling "consumed" by our thoughts. In the Taittiriya Upanishad, one of the sacred books of the Hindus, the world as nourisher and nourished, devourer and devoured, is summed up:

> *From food all creatures are produced*
> *And all creatures that dwell on earth*
> *By food they live*
> *And into food they finally pass.*
> *Food is the chief among beings. . . .*
> *Verily he obtains all food*
> *Who worships the Divine as food.*

Here we see that the ultimate food is to experience all creation, even divinity itself, as that which is fed upon, consumed with delight, and longed for again and again. Nothing is to remain undigested because it is our deepest nature to fully consume life and, in turn, to be life's food.

## KEY LESSONS

- Seeing through the eyes of fear distorts our perceptions and causes us to act out paradoxical eating behaviors.

- We often reach for food as a symbolic substitute for love.

- Food *is* a faithful resource for love, but things become problematic when we expect food to compensate for a lack of love.

- Because we see things metaphorically, food does not appear simply as food. To a dieter food looks like fat, to an athlete muscle, to a scientist chemicals, to an invalid medicine.

- "Nourishment" is one of the primary metaphors through which we view the world. Nothing escapes eating and nothing escapes being eaten.

REFLECTIONS

- When did you begin to feel embarrassed about your body, your nakedness? What change happened inside you? Why is it a child does not fear nakedness but adults do?

- How would your life change if you believed that your body and mind were fine as they are, that nothing was "wrong" with you? Is this condition possible? Do you want it to be possible?

- Can you recall times when you have chased after impossible goals? What were they? Why would you pursue something you knew you could not attain? What part of you does this feed?

- Are you working on solving any problems in your life? Have you ever asked yourself if these problems are real?

- Do you substitute food for love? Which foods are your favorites? What are the short-term effects of this substitution? Long-term? How can you make substitutes truly work for you? How can you get what you really want without substitutes?

- The world is constantly eating itself—plants eat the soil, animals eat the plants, people eat the plants and animals, and the earth swallows everything. Where do you fit into this process? Can you picture yourself in the great food chain? Does this perspective change the way you see yourself as an eater?

- Where does your food come from? Who manufactures it? Who grew it? Are the ingredients good quality? Do you think these questions are important?

- Where do your ideas about food come from? Who manufactured them? Exactly why do you like some foods and not others?

- Observe children eating. Note their mannerisms and attitude. Does their experience of eating seem different from yours? Do children enjoy eating?

- The next time you eat, pretend you are a child.

# 8

# Body Image

J ust as we use food as a substitute for love and nourishment, so do we use body image as a substitute for body reality. Because we are seldom fully satisfied with what we have, we naturally want the body to be different, to conform to the standards we believe will ensure love and acceptance from others. Body image is a mental snapshot we hold of our body overlaid with a complex of feelings, judgments, and fantasies. Stated in another way, body image is how we imagine our body together with the emotional repercussions of that imagining.

We may wake up one morning feeling very good about ourselves and about how we look. This is often called a "positive" body image. We may awaken the next morning feeling unhappy with life and with our appearance and hence have a "negative" body image. The body has not changed at all. Our mental state has.

Someone with an "ideal" body could have a negative

body image, while someone whom others might consider physically unappealing could have a very positive body image. Believe it or not, physical appearance has little to do with body image. It is the *self*-image that determines our body image. Who we are inside and how content we are determine the degree to which we accept our body. I have often watched women who have dieted and achieved their ideal body weight or men who have exercised and achieved their desired build, whose body image remained negative. They continued to compare themselves to others and lived in fear of losing what they had achieved. Their bodies had changed but their self-image remained the same. Looking in the mirror they saw an improved physique, but looking within they saw the same unworthy self.

Few people see the body as it really is but imagine what they would like it to be. The fantasy of an ideal body comes with the false promise of eternal happiness and unconditional acceptance by others. The instant we create this ideal image, we begin to feed it, nurture it, and reinforce it as if it were real. We stop living life fully now and wait for a future condition we may never attain.

The secret to creating a healthy body image is, in principle, very simple—acceptance. Acceptance of what is, acceptance of our limitations, and acceptance that an ideal appearance does not guarantee happiness anyway. Yes, it is true that people with a certain kind of look tend to be more accepted and sought after by others. But why let that ruin your life? There is nothing wrong with having an image of a body we desire more and working to create that kind of body. The secret is not investing that image with the exclusive ability to bring us happiness.

## Nutrition, Imagination, and the Body

Bodies are not simply biological facts, static anatomical entities that obey scientific laws alone. Bodies are imagined. We may imagine them walking over red hot coals, running, biking, and swimming consecutively for hundreds of miles, being healed with needle insertions according to invisible acupuncture meridian maps, or responding "miraculously" to the channeled energy of faith healers or the rituals of a shaman. The way we imagine the body is a foundation for how it responds physiologically.

Likewise, the way we imagine the body will determine our relationship to food, the types of food we eat, and the kind of body we will help create. For example, if we imagine our body to be a necessary nuisance, a piece of luggage we are obligated to drag along, we will likely view diet and nutrition in a similar fashion. Nourishing the body will be treated as a chore, and healthy eating will be unappealing. Because we help create biologically the type of body we imagine psychologically, it is not uncommon for those who imagine their body as cumbersome to reach for foods that enhance the condition of sluggishness and heaviness in the body—excessively fatty foods and high caloric meals.

If we imagine the body differently, for example as if it were an important piece of athletic machinery to be well maintained and fine-tuned, we would reach for a completely different diet, perhaps one that includes vitamin supplements, health foods, and meals designed for their digestive efficiency. Over time these foods would help create a body very different from our previous example, one that is leaner, more energetic, and better nourished. And this difference in biology originates simply by imagining the body in a different way.

For many people gender plays an important role in how we imagine the body and the diet we subsequently create. It is certainly no secret that women and men see body and diet differently and that both sexes have unique approaches to food that generate some fascinating behaviors. What are the nuances of the male mind and female mind that influence our relationship to food? And from whence do they arise?

## Feminine Images

If Freud had been a woman, psychoanalysis would have been founded upon our relationship to food and nourishment rather than the sexual drive. The reason is this: The drive in women to nourish and their role as nourisher is as powerful and psychologically significant as the drive in men to procreate. Freud quite naturally saw through the perspective of his gender, describing the psyche in terms of the libido, the male libido in particular. Rather than detail the symbolic significance of the phallus, a female Freud would have described the symbolism of food, the dynamics of the mother-daughter relationship, and a psychology based on our earliest experiences of eating.

Indeed, it can be argued that the way we learn about life from our earliest moments centers around eating. The child learns about pleasure when it receives milk, and pain when milk is absent. It struggles for autonomy as it learns to handle a spoon and demand the food it wants. And much of this learning revolves around the mother. It is the mother who carries us inside her, nurses us in her arms, cooks for us in her kitchen, and provides the matrix of nourishment and support through which we gradually learn autonomy in the world.

Women and food share an intimate relationship. It is no secret that civilizations past have worshipped the Goddess and revered the Earth Mother. And it is no coincidence that the current renaissance in America of rediscovering the Goddess has coincided with peak interest in food and nutrition, and a surge in the occurrence and acknowledgment of eating disorders. By contacting the divinity of the Goddess, we also unearth her diseases. As more and more women are breaking free of traditionally feminine roles and experimenting with new identities and new powers in a rapidly changing world, eating disorders appear as a woman's unique way of expressing her confusion and struggle. An entire generation of women is moving into uncharted territory. I firmly believe that the anorexics, bulimics, and chronic dieters of today can teach us as much about the psyche and the direction in which we are heading as hysterics taught Freud and schizophrenics taught Jung.

Because of a woman's close connection to food, she is likely to express her longing for love and struggle for selfhood through eating. Whereas men are traditionally encouraged to "find themselves" out in the world, women are traditionally encouraged to achieve selfhood in the home, the kitchen, and at the table. When a woman chronically diets or an anorexic attempts to starve herself of food, what she is really starving for is meaning, the meaning of being a woman in a culture where the messages about what this means are distorted and confused. And perhaps the biggest confusion occurs in body image.

For many women eating is directly linked to body weight. Food does not so much look like food anymore, it looks like fat. Because fat is said to have over twice as many calories as the same amount of protein or carbohydrates, fat becomes a substance to be feared. Meals are judged by calorie content and their potential to make the body bigger. A woman once told me that before she eats a meal, she automatically imagines the places on her body, usually hips and stomach, that will fatten. Because her goal of eating (and of life) is to be thin, she spends more energy imagining the horrors the food will do to her than simply eating and enjoying. Food is reduced to a cosmetic. The word *cosmetic* is derived from the Greek root *kosmos* meaning "order," "form," "skillful arrangement," "the universe," and when seeing things cosmetically we concentrate only on the surface, reducing the expanse of the cosmos (and the body's place in it) to just the skin. With this emphasis on surfaces, the inside of things naturally loses its meaning. Thus we often describe those preoccupied with their outer appearance as "shallow," "lacking depth," or "superficial." Their consciousness is quite literally focused on one small layer of existence—they do more to improve how they look and less to improve who they are. In addition, because the inside is de-emphasized, whatever goes into the body—food, drugs, alcohol, or cigarette smoke—does not matter; that is, as matter, these substances are not seen to affect the body. Even when cosmetically oriented people do positive things for the body, it is seldom done out of love for health but rather out of fear of not looking good.

They imagine the appearance of the body to be crucial to social acceptance and hence to self-love. Because the ego can never be fully satisfied we often try to look different, comparing our physical features to those around us with detailed mental lists of who is better and why we have come up short. Without the right body we feel apart from "the real life," excluded from the happiness experienced by beautiful people.

The woman who desperately seeks slenderness is attempting to embody the qualities of mature womanhood—nurturance, earthiness, sensuality, femininity, and spiritual connectedness—through a quick-fix method. She expects to incorporate these through outer development alone. Ironically, by becoming excessively slender she creates the opposite effect—an adolescent-type body reminiscent of a teenager rather than an empowered woman. And most tellingly, she develops an adolescent attitude by substituting body image for self-image, by hoping that her deepest needs in life will be met by looking right rather than being right.

When we minimize our intake of food or see only fat when looking at a meal, we symbolically remove "nourishment" from eating. And if we do this with food, we are no doubt removing the nourishing qualities from life as well, shielding ourselves from intimacy, companionship, and joy. Food is not the problem; it is only an indication of a deeper yearning. And yet the more a woman attempts to feed that deeper yearning through thinness, the more she starves. Though she seeks true nourishment and wants to find loving friends and relationships, she inevitably attracts those who are similar to herself, self-absorbed and concerned with appearance.

Such a woman hopes to create a state of no change, for once we attain the bodily state we desire, we have symbolically gained control over the unknown, or so we believe. A thin body that stays the same, that does not fill out with changes in the seasons, body cycles, age, maturity, or even pregnancy, represents our ability to control, to conquer the forces we fear most: physical deterioration, uncertainty, and death.

In extreme cases some women seek control of their fate by literally starving away their problem, in this case, the body. We call these people anorexics. Anorexics seek to create a body that needs no nourishment, be it food, intimacy, or any outside care, a body that exists in a state of false equilibrium, completely thin, predictable, and self-sustaining. I visited one eighty-five-pound anorexic woman who was hospitalized in intensive care; she would not eat. She stood in front of a full-length mirror, and I asked her what she saw. She replied, "A fat person." Here was the skinniest woman I had ever seen, a warm, bright, articulate, college-educated lady, telling me that she was fat. Several months later she died. What affected me so deeply was that she had convinced herself that she was seeing something that was just not there, a tragic misperception that killed her. Can you imagine, then, the little ways we fool ourselves when we look in the mirror and miss the beauty that is there, or look upon another and see whom we imagine rather than the person truly before us.

It should be noted that even women who have bodies that many of us would consider ideal will nevertheless look in the mirror and wish for something different. They feel unattractive because they hold the fundamental belief that "I am not enough." They look around and find someone to measure themselves against and invariably come up short. No matter how beautiful we are or how skilled in a particular area, there is always someone better. And yet we can never really be sure of our comparisons because even though someone looks better, we do not honestly know if they *feel* better. We have little idea what their life is like or how content they are with the qualities we covet so dearly.

In one well-publicized story, the popular talk show host Oprah Winfrey went on an intensive medically supervised fast to lose weight. She openly discussed how she wanted to look good and feel better about herself. When she unveiled her new and slender self before millions of viewers, she made a particularly revealing comment. She mentioned that her biggest fear was that she would gain the weight back. Can you imagine the pressure she faced? She'd lost weight to feel better about life but was living in fear that millions of people would see her strategy backfire? If the motivation to lose weight is out of fear of not being good enough, then even if the weight is lost, we will still be in fear and, as in Oprah Winfrey's case, perhaps even more fear than we began with. So what starts out as a strategy to feel better by being thinner results in our feeling worse. Ultimately, then, it is the fear of not being a worthy and lovable person that we want to lose; the weight is merely secondary.

## Masculine Images

As the cultural image of the female body shrinks, the cultural image of the male body swells. For many men food is also directly linked to weight, but whereas a woman sees fat when looking at food, a man sees protein, the potential for food to add muscle weight to his body. The cosmetically oriented male is characterized by the weight lifter who uses an increase in muscularity (physical power) as a substitute for inner power. A strong body equals a strong self-image equals reverence from others. The man looks to protein, the structural element of both muscle and bone tissue, to increase his manliness. Because he sees the world as a competitive arena, he wants to be bigger, stronger, more aggressive. With these comes a protection from the world, yet an access to it, an access through the embodiment of a desirable male image. Ironically, the very qualities such a man seeks to create are often distorted into a kind of armor, the build-up of muscle tissue to shield one from the world and to block the flow of emotional and creative expression.

A favorite ritual of those who take this approach is the eating contest. Here a group of men will either compete directly with each other to see who can eat the most or simply take casual delight among themselves in eating large amounts. On one level the man in the eating contest eats huge amounts to show he can "take anything." He is making a symbolic statement: "I am strong, unemotional, unmoved, and untouched by nourishment." Remember that *food* represents everything that *nourishment* means. Instead of the man saying, "I am unable and afraid to receive love, intimacy, and nourishment," he says, "Look everybody! I can eat huge amounts of nourishment and not feel a thing!" Invulnerability to food equals invulnerability to feelings, which of course equals "manliness." Instead of being a substance to enjoy and be nourished by, food is reduced to its opposite: a hardening agent, a toughening routine. On an even deeper level the man uses food to assert his dominion over the body. By eating huge amounts he has symbolically conquered the forces of nature and proved that he alone (and not the laws of the universe) is in control. He believes the body is invincible and will not die.

A close cousin of this game is the drinking contest. The difference here is that alcohol has a very obvious range of effects. In small quantities it can be a pleasant potion. In large amounts it can be a poison. By drinking huge amounts men are challenging and defying their bodies, trying to prove themselves masters of it. "Let's see who can make themselves the sickest, most nauseated, most uncoordinated, yet still be *in control.*" The drinking contest is a ritual passage into manhood. Its basic premise is that abusing the body makes it better, worthy, and immortal (that is, no pain, no gain). To validate himself, the man must first abuse his body through eating, drinking, exercising, or competition. Then he must prevent pain and emotion from being expressed.

Note that in the drinking contest the man abuses through unrestrained drinking and controls by suppressing the urge to vomit. In the eating disorder of bulimia (bingeing and purging) the woman abuses through unrestrained eating and controls by willful vomiting. Another intriguing comparison of men and women is that in the eating contest men openly compete to see who can eat more, while a common habit among women is to compete secretly to see who can eat less.

Just as men and women use diet to emphasize their particular concepts of maleness and femaleness, they also use it to de-emphasize sexuality and gender-related traits. For example, rather than eat less food to enhance the desirability of the body, some women eat more food to deflect others from their body. The more weight they carry, the more they are shielded from the world, from men, and from their own sexuality. Food becomes a vehicle for rebelliousness, a way to say no to life. Of course a woman can have a large body and be very much in tune with her sexuality and open to the world. In contrast, one can have a physically beautiful appearance yet be asexual and inhibited. Ultimately, it is the inner attitude that enlivens the body and gives us the power to attract.

It is interesting to note that in contrast to women who use excess food and body weight to hide sexuality and feminine expression, some men use a lack of food and decreased body weight to deny their masculine side. The "disappearing man," as I call him, is afraid to be male and hence shuns such qualities as strength, dominance, action, and aggression. He is confused and dissatisfied with the ideal images that society attaches to men: the violent macho style, the sexual hype, and the cool unemotional mask. He lacks effective role models and feels alone in his symbolic journey into manhood. Consequently, he takes what seems to be the best available option: He chooses not to be a man.

The disappearing man uses food to manifest his internal psychological state. He eats very little and creates a body that is slender or frail. His appetite decreases because for a man, to eat is symbolically to become more embodied, more alive, stronger, and more "male." In denying the masculine element his female characteristics are therefore emphasized. He feels emotionally vulnerable, more comfortable around women (or like-minded men), and may even have an open dislike for "hard males."

One man recounted his experience: "During high school most of my friends were women. I felt more in touch with them. I didn't relate to the guys very well; most of them seemed out of touch or a little too unfeeling. I was a good athlete and played on the baseball team but still felt an outcast around other men. When I graduated from high school

I began to eat less, and in a few years my weight dropped from 160 to 135. I certainly felt lighter, more gentle, and as I look back on it now, very much the way I imagine a woman would feel. Eventually, I joined a hiking club in college that turned out to be all men. We grew very close, and my experience with them helped me to see how much I had pushed men out of life, especially the man within me. . . . I didn't even make this connection until later on, but as I began to contact that lost part of myself, I started eating more. I gained back the weight I had lost after high school. It felt good to be strong again and this may sound strange, but it was as if I was becoming a man for the first time. . . ."

It is fascinating to note how men eat more to emphasize masculinity and less to de-emphasize it, while women eat less to enhance femininity and more to hide it. Can you see how our feelings about sexuality and the different roles expected of the sexes affect our relationship to food? Do you see how we use diet to help create the kind of body that is in line with how we view the world?

## KEY LESSONS

- We often use body image as a substitute for body reality.

- The secret to creating a healthy body image is simple and straightforward—acceptance.

- The way we imagine the body helps determine our relationship to eating, the foods we reach for, and the body we create.

- Because of a woman's intimate connection to food and nurturance she is likely to express her longing for love and struggle for selfhood through eating.

- When women are preoccupied with weight, food looks like fat. When men are preoccupied with strength, food looks like protein.

- Women often lose weight to enhance sexuality and gain weight to hide it, while men gain weight to enhance sexuality, and lose weight to hide it.

### REFLECTIONS

- Where does your body image come from? Has your body image changed in the course of your life? In what ways? Why did it change? Who changed it?

- Think of someone who is very overweight. Imagine you are that person. How do you feel about yourself? How do you think other people see you? Think of someone with the looks and body you would love to have and imagine you are that person. How do you see yourself? How do others see you? Now imagine that each of these people is imagining he or she has your body and looks. How do they see themselves? How would life change for them?

- Why are there more female anorexics and bulimics than males? Why are more and more teenage and preadolescent girls starving themselves in order to be thinner?

- Go to your local library and compare the paintings of Degas, Picasso, Giorgione, Rembrandt, Botticelli, Leonardo da Vinci, Maxfield Parrish, Andy Warhol, and the drawings in Marvel comic books. What can you tell about how each of these artists sees the female body?

*For Women*

- What do you see when you look at food? Do you see fat? Calories? Does your limited vision of food inhibit a full and joyous experience of eating? What do you need to change inside yourself to see food as it really is?

- Exactly what would be the benefits if you looked just the way you wanted to? Are these benefits truly important to you? Do you need to wait until you are thin to have them? What would it take for you to accept and love your body as it is?

- For one week observe how men relate to food. Observe their mannerisms and attitudes. Do you notice any differences? What can this teach you about men? What can this teach you about yourself?

- For one day pretend you are a man when you eat. Have the attitude that you think a man has when he eats. Note any reactions and insights.

- Exactly how do you think men consider you when they watch you eat? When they look at your body? Do you feel certain this is what they think? Have you ever asked anyone to see if it is true? Is it possible that men are not thinking what you think they're thinking?

*For Men*

- How would you benefit from looking the way you want? Are these benefits truly important to you? Can you bring these benefits into your life right now?

- How does your desire for a stronger or more beautiful body stop you from living life? Is your body image tied to your self-image? Does the way you feel about your body affect how you experience your masculinity? Your relationship to food?

- Is your body's nourishment a priority? How does it compare to other priorities? What would you do if you were to nourish your body more fully?

- Are there ways in which you abuse your body? What is the payoff for doing so? The drawbacks?

- For one week notice the ways in which a woman relates to food. Do you see any interesting differences? What can this teach you about women? About yourself?

- For one day pretend you are a woman when you eat. Assume the attitude of a woman when she eats. Note any reactions and insights.

# 9

# *The Nature of Habits*

Habits are the core of our relationship to food, the behaviors that determine the quality of our experience with eating. For many of us the eating experience is a problematic one because we cannot make lasting changes in our everyday habits. As Mark Twain once said about habits, "Quitting smoking is the easiest thing in the world. I should know. I've done it over ten thousand times."

Habits are thoughts or activities that are repeated over and over either in an unconscious and mechanical fashion or through willful effort. The word *habit* often holds a negative connotation. However, it has a brighter and more complete perspective. The mind is, by nature, habitual. Each of us has an inborn, habit-forming process that helps us with a most important task—learning. Have you ever observed a small child learn something new? When I played peekaboo with my five-month-old nephew, covering my eyes and then pulling my hands away, he laughed with excitement. I imagined that after six or seven peekaboos the humor would wear off, but he wanted to see it again and again, laughing each time. Peekaboo was more than just a game; my nephew was learning object constancy. To an infant's mind, when a ball disappears behind a couch or eyes disappear behind hands, they are gone forever. Seeing my face return was a humorous and fascinating experience because what he thought was supposed to happen—face disappear into oblivion—did not. And he wanted to see it over and over because human beings learn through repetition. The nervous system is programmed to learn important information by repeating it. How many times will a child sing the ABC song in its zest for learning? And how many times will we, as adults, make the same mistakes in life until we learn our lesson?

The process of habituating, of repeating something over and over, essentially serves one purpose—to move us toward that which brings pleasure and away from that which brings pain. The learning process is naturally pleasurable, so we will instinctively repeat any learning behavior that provides us with more knowledge and control of our environment. This process of the repetition of pleasure is easily distorted. For example, at some time in the past we may have come home from school or work after a distressing day, had some ice cream, and felt better almost immediately. The mind then quietly recorded, "Feel bad, eat ice cream, feel good." During similar situations, the mind will automatically repeat this useful and accurate observation, and thus a habit is born. We have secured pleasure while avoiding pain.

## The Two Types of Habits

Habits are divided into two categories: positive and negative. The words *positive* and *negative* are not moral judgments as to the inherent goodness or evilness of a habit but rather neutral terms describing the effects of these habits, assessments of the quality of experience and biological consequences the habit evokes. A negative habit is a behavior that is repeated mechanically and automatically. It drains or disperses our energy, has harmful repercussions on the body or emotions, and goes against what we want most for ourselves.

Characteristically, negative habits have some immediate positive or pleasurable benefits; however, these benefits are short-lived and may eventually yield harmful consequences. An example of a negative habit is excessive smoking. Smoking a cigarette gives people the immediate benefit of calmness and emotional security. Over time an increased amount of cigarette smoking is needed to provide the same effect, and if this habit is repeated often enough, shortness of breath, congestion, and lung disease may result. So the same part of the mind that automatically replays, "Feel bad, smoke cigarette, feel good" is *not* the part of us that can evaluate the continued usefulness of this habit, for without self-reflection and intervention, our mechanical nature will dominate. The distinguishing feature of negative habits is that they come naturally, take little effort to develop, and quickly gain a momentum of their own that is difficult to offset. Few people have a problem in starting a sweet tooth or an overeating habit.

Positive habits, on the other hand, generally need to be cultivated, nurtured, and given constant effort to make them mainstays in our life. Positive habits enhance and support the body's functions, serve the mind and emotions, and bring lasting benefits with little or no harmful side effects. As we cultivate a positive habit, it, too, gains a momentum of its own and grows easier to practice, especially as we begin to notice the benefits it brings. For example, years ago, at the urging of my dentist, I decided to begin regular daily flossing. Despite my initial resistance it seemed like a smart idea for the long-term health of my teeth. The first few weeks were traumatic; the floss broke and stuck between my teeth, my gums bled, and some teeth did not have enough space between them to pull the floss through. However, I stayed with it and soon noticed some benefits: My teeth looked better, my mouth felt cleaner, and I was feeling great self-satisfaction. A positive habit was born.

In addition to direct benefits, positive habits also yield "cross benefits," additional improvements that occur without effort. For instance, aside from the usual benefits of regular exercise, people often report it inspires other positive habits, such as eating healthier foods and cutting down on drinking and smoking. Once we practice one positive habit, the desire to do more positive things increases.

It is no secret that habits are hard to control. Most people who lose weight gain it back because they change their habits while on the diet but revert back to the old way of eating when off the diet. Likewise, people with the goal of healthy eating may eat sensibly for a week and then suddenly binge on forbidden foods. They devise a method for short-term change of habits but have no long-term strategies. Others may have simple habits they wish to alter—overeating or indulging in too much sugar or coffee—yet their efforts are futile.

Why are habits so difficult to work with? Are we stuck with our habits for life? Can we do anything to change them? Many of us have already tried the most habitual and least successful way to change a habit—fighting it. Indeed, the complaint I hear most often about habits is, "I have habits that won't change no matter how hard I fight them. I just don't have the willpower." And these people are absolutely correct. They do not have enough willpower because the type of willpower they employ can never be enough. They are using the wrong kind.

## Negative Willpower

What most people call willpower is a negative force. Negative willpower is the use of fear, tension, and aggression to fight a habit. It is an attempt to address a habit by bulldozing it into oblivion. Because we have convinced ourselves that having a habit is bad, the most logical strategy seems to be the overpowering of the habit by force. Ironically, negative willpower fails for these two reasons: (1) Fighting a habit makes the habit stronger; (2) Hating or fearing a habit further binds us to it.

Think back for a moment to any habit you have tried to change but could not. Did you think of the habit as bad or evil? What methods did you employ to overcome the habit? Did you fight it? Do you recall your frustration and anxiety in trying to defeat the habit? Did the habit seem to grow stronger and more formidable as you fought it? Did you make a gallant effort to suppress your urges but then give in because you hadn't enough willpower?

When we use negative willpower to fight a habit, the habit automatically fights back with an equal and opposite force. The more we fight, the more the habit resists, and the greater our entrenchment in it. You have probably noticed that when someone orders you to do something you do not want to do, you inwardly resist or outwardly rebel. You might even be ordered to do something you *do* want to do but resist anyway because someone ordered you to do it. The same dynamic happens in the mind. By attempting to overcome a part of yourself with force, *you* do not like it so *you* fight back. It seems as if different people are fighting, but it is the same person. It is as if one of your hands were wrestling with the other. No matter which one wins, you lose.

Occasionally we *can* overcome a habit by fighting it with negative willpower. Yet the victory is short-lived, and the habit returns because it was only temporarily overwhelmed by strength, or the habit is re-formed into another, equally damaging habit. This last point is an important one in understanding the habit-changing process. We are setting our sights on *transforming* habits, not *re-forming* them. A habit is re-formed when we use negative willpower to suppress the habit. Even though it appears to be eliminated, we have not transformed it, but simply pushed it down into the unconscious, an act of temporary disappearance. Eventually the habit resurfaces when it has found a new outlet. Hence drug addicts who overcome their habit through fighting it often become alcoholics, and many alcoholics who have defeated their addiction become sugar junkies, coffee addicts, or overeaters. They have traded one addiction for another, which is the real definition of a "re-formed" addict—someone who has re-created their addiction under a new name.

The strength of a habit increases when we fight it because we are trying to suppress the urge behind the habit. Every habit has within it a natural urge that seeks expression. The habit of drinking has the natural urge within it to feel the pleasurable effects that the substance alcohol has on the nervous system. The habit of overeating contains the natural urge for the experience of satiation. The same applies for sugar, coffee, tobacco, or narcotics. Each fulfills a different bioemotional urge. These urges are natural, sensible, and real, and there is nothing wrong or problematic about them. It is the habit or addiction we create around the urge that causes us trouble.

For example, the habit of eating excessive sugar contains the natural urge for the bioemotional experience of sweetness. This urge must be either expressed at its fundamental level by eating something sweet, or transformed to another level by experiencing satisfaction through creative outlets, such as music, movement, et cetera. Suppressing this urge by fighting it with negative willpower closes off not only the outlet of eating sweet foods, which seemingly solves the problem of the habit, but also closes off other outlets as well. Selective shut-down is not possible. If we close off from someone we love—a parent, friend, or lover—because they hurt us, we invariably close off from others as well. The same occurs when we block a natural urge.

And what we experience as a growing urge for sugar is really the buildup of tension from artificially suppressing the urge. Eventually we may explode from this bottled-up tension and either go on a sugar binge or re-form the urge into a new habit. I am not implying that we cater to whatever urges arise. I am simply noting that suppression creates tension, and that at least half of the power of a habit is the degree to which we fear and fight it.

## Positive Willpower

The key to changing a habit is positive willpower. Positive willpower *accepts* a habit and transforms it with a force that is directed by intelligence. Negative willpower is like a monkey with a hammer. The monkey has the strength to hit a nail, but without the know-how it will hammer everything in sight. Positive willpower is that same hammer in the hands of a human being, a primate with intelligence. This intelligence directs our efforts and helps us achieve our goals with a minimum of energy. It inspires patience, persistence, and focus.

Two patients I worked with in a cardiac support group were recovering from mild heart attacks. They were instructed to follow a therapeutic diet that would help lower their blood pressure and serum cholesterol.

Richard was grateful to have survived his heart attack and eager to eliminate slowly from his diet those foods that were risk-inducing as he began to include more of those that were risk-reducing. He was able to make major changes in his habitual way of eating with the least amount of stress.

Albert, on the other hand, feared another heart attack and was horrified at the thought of being an invalid. Albert was not running toward life—he was running away from death.

Like Richard, Albert followed a standard American diet; however, he feared it would be impossible to change. Albert loved his cold cuts and his salty foods and was doubtful he could renounce his nightly urge for a Carvel ice-cream float. He decided the only way to manage the new diet was to go cold turkey, to drop all the old foods and adopt the new ones overnight. He tried to fight his old way of eating and, not surprisingly, lost the battle. Within a month he left the cardiac program.

Many people are unable to accept their habits, and this lack of acceptance inhibits the transformation process. Acceptance is always the first step. Then we need to remember to work *for* something, not *against* it. This is the difference between positive and negative willpower.

Observe what happens when a small child is learning to walk. Because the child learns through trial and error, the parents do not yell or hit the child over the head if it falls down. They do not say, "We do not accept you; we want a better baby that already knows how to walk." They simply laugh and encourage the child to try again. And after the briefest upset the child forgets its uncoordination and happily begins again as if for the first time. Consider yourself that same child in your efforts to change a habit.

As you work with your habits, observe the type of willpower you employ. Cultivate positive willpower by remembering the following points: (1) Accept your habit and transform it with an attitude of love rather than fear; (2) Regulate a habit by confronting it with centered strength rather than overpowering it with fighting and suppression; (3) Be persistent, dedicated, and one-pointed in your efforts; (4) When all your efforts fail and you find yourself succumbing to an eating habit, relax, enjoy yourself, and try again the next time.

## KEY LESSONS

- The mind is, by nature, habitual. Negative habits are automatic and mechanical and yield undesirable consequences. Positive habits yield desirable benefits and generally require cultivation.

- When we experience something as pleasurable, we will attempt to repeat it and control it; yet when we become dependent on that source of pleasure, we are essentially "out of control."

- Negative willpower is the use of fear and tension to fight a habit. Positive willpower is the use of force plus intelligence and enthusiasm.

- What is often experienced as a growing urge for a food is really the build-up of tension from artificially suppressing the urge.

- Accepting a habit is the first step to changing it.

## REFLECTIONS

- Exactly what do you control in life? How do you control it? Why do you control it? Can you really control anything?

- List as many of your negative habits as you can think of. What are the immediate benefits of these habits? What are the long-term drawbacks? Do you fight these habits? What practical steps can you take to manage them more effectively?

- List as many of your positive habits as you can think of. How do these habits benefit you? Are they easy to practice? Do you enjoy practicing them? Do you think more about your negative habits than your positive ones? If so, how can you give yourself more credit for the good things you do?

- Gandhi once said, "Hate the sin but love the sinner." Think of a habit you have that you aren't fond of. For one week practice loving yourself even though you have an unwanted habit.

- Think of a habit someone else has that you are not fond of. For one week practice loving them even though they have a habit you don't like.

- Think of a habit you would like to change. List all the factors that would help you change this habit. List all the factors that would hinder you. Then try to change the habit.

- Choose a positive habit you'd like to have. List all the factors that would help you develop this habit. List all the factors that would hinder you. Then cultivate the habit.

# 10

## *Cravings*

Years ago, while preparing my master's thesis on psychology and nutrition, I had a fascinating encounter with a craving. During several months of intensive day and night writing I would break at six each evening, drive to a local store, and purchase a pint of homemade vanilla ice cream and two bran muffins. This was all I ate for dinner each day. Toward the final days of my work I noticed that not only did I enjoy the bran muffins and ice cream, but I craved them. I realized I could not get through the day without my fix. Here I was writing about psychology and nutrition and I was addicted to bran muffins and ice cream.

One evening I tried an experiment. I decided to see what would happen if I did not give in to my craving. I sat on the couch, looked out the window, and agreed to stay there until the craving was gone. But the longer I sat, the stronger it grew, and the more convinced I became that I should end the experiment. But I stayed. I sat, I took deep breaths, I watched my anxiety grow deeper, and as the overwhelming impulse to eat bran muffins and ice cream peaked, as the longing and pain consumed my entire body, I burst into tears, convulsed on the couch, and sobbed uncontrollably.

I do not know how long I sat and cried, but sometime later I realized I was peacefully looking out the window, watching the birds and the tall grass, deeply relaxed and content. I had been in another world. Why was I so relaxed? Had I fallen asleep? I remembered the craving episode but it had gone without a trace. Bran muffins and ice cream seemed like a distant memory. I had no more desire for them, nor have I craved them since.

What happened? How did the craving disappear? Why did it appear in the first place? Many people I speak with are mystified by the intensity of their cravings. They believe that they desire certain foods because their body has an important nutritional need, while cravings for other foods arise from some unnatural process and that those foods would indeed harm the body. Are there really "good" and "bad" cravings, and if so, how can we tell the difference? We can answer these questions and unravel the mystery of the bran-muffins-and-ice-cream incident by first looking at the three kinds of cravings.

## Supportive Cravings

For general purposes cravings can be divided into three types: supportive, dispersive, and associative. A supportive craving occurs when the body instinctively yearns for a food that enhances the healing process, fulfills a nutritional need, or neutralizes an imbalance in the body. Have you ever noticed some of the peculiar things pets eat when sick? Cats may chew on plants and grasses, dogs may eat old pinecones and pieces of wood or lick clay deposits. No one tells a dog to eat clay because the positively charged minerals it contains helps neutralize acidic poisons in its system and shifts blood pH back to normal, nor would the dog understand if anyone did. It is acting upon an instinctive process far beyond reason. The same process occurs in human beings.

Supportive cravings may arise that seem sensible and obvious or unexpected and beyond nutritional understanding. For example, some people crave citrus foods when suffering from a cold or the flu, a not unnatural desire considering the vitamin C content of oranges and grapefruits and the cleansing effect of fruit on the body. Other cravings defy traditional understanding but prove remarkably successful. Some examples I have observed include raspberry juice for headache and fatigue, fresh figs for depression, and peanut butter for nasal congestion. These cravings are unique to the individuals who experience them and would probably prove useless for most others.

## Dispersive Cravings

A dispersive craving is a desire for a food that drains our health and disperses body energy. Though the intensity of a dispersive desire may be as strong as the intensity of a supportive one, the ultimate effects of yielding to dispersive cravings are detrimental. Many of us long for foods we know have adverse reactions on the body when eaten in excess: sugar, alcohol, caffeine. How is it that we can crave something beneficial, yet also crave something harmful? If the body is so naturally wise, how could it make such foolish mistakes? The answer lies in the nature of yearning.

Life itself is a yearning. We yearn for meaning, purpose, love, and the fulfillment of our dreams. Behind every human act, no matter how singular or small, is a yearning for more, more life, more depth of experience. Through the many difficulties and obstacles we face, our yearnings may become distorted. The natural yearning for inner strength may become a compulsion for power over others. The yearning for love may be turned into a hopeless attempt to gain approval from everyone we meet. Or the yearning for self-fulfillment may become an obsession to accumulate money and prestige.

The body also yearns. It yearns for food, water, touch, sound, and sensuality. It yearns for aliveness through sweet things, tasty things, and whatever stimulates and excites the senses to a heightened experience of life. The body yearns for more of itself. And just as psychological yearnings can become distorted, so can biological ones. A dispersive craving is a distorted yearning in the body. The body is literally fooled into thinking that excessive consumption of harmful substances would be helpful.

Stated in another way, we often yearn for experiences in life we firmly believe are needed. We may pursue a friendship, relationship, job, or any course of action that seems to be the right direction at the time but later proves to be wrong. The body is equally blind when confronted with powerful substances or experiences that promise fulfillment: alcohol, sugar, caffeine. These substances seem to be the correct choices, but when the negative consequences of overconsumption are experienced, we learn their true nature.

## Associative Cravings

The third type of craving is called an associative craving. In one sense it is a cross between the other two. It occurs when we yearn for a food that has a rich, deep, and meaningful association with our past. For example, many people report that when visiting their parents or grandparents they automatically long for foods from their childhood even though those foods are not a regular part of their diet. One middle-aged woman craves spaghetti and meatballs whenever she visits her elderly mother. If she did not see her mother, she wouldn't even think of this dish. Yet each time her childhood memories are sparked, and she explains that "it feels as though my taste buds step into a time machine."

A friend of mine suddenly found himself wanting bagels with cream cheese and butter. He had never before eaten this combination of foods, nor did it seem appealing when he thought about it. He realized later that this was his father's favorite food, and the desire had arisen at a time when he was going through an unexpected period of longing for his father, who had died a decade earlier. On a symbolic level bagels with cream cheese and butter *was* his father, and in eating this food he was reincorporating his father into his life.

A host of different circumstances can trigger an associative craving. Once, while on a seven-day fast, I spontaneously began to long for foods I had not eaten since childhood, particularly Marshmallow Fluff with peanut butter and grilled cheese sandwiches. Several days after these desires subsided I was suddenly struck by the thought, "I want chocolate Maypo." It sounded like nonsense to me because I did not know what Maypo was, nor could I be certain that it came in chocolate if it existed. Yet I was craving a distinct taste and couldn't get chocolate Maypo out of my mind. Later on I questioned my mother and learned that chocolate Maypo had been my favorite food when I was three and that I especially enjoyed the television commercial for Maypo because the cartoon character, Marky Maypo, had the same first name as I did. To this day I still cannot recall eating it as a child, nor am I convinced that anyone named Marky Maypo ever existed.

Associative cravings are often the most difficult to deal with because we're uncertain about whether they are beneficial or not. For instance, the foods we desire from our childhood may be of little nutritional value, yet eating them might bring such satisfaction and warm feelings that it might not be worth resisting. A woman who was on a fairly strict health-food/weight-loss diet began having a constant craving for Aunt Jemima pancakes with maple syrup and butter. She had many memories of this breakfast food from her childhood, and eating it brought her great joy. Yet it clearly conflicted with her diet. It was fattening and unhealthy. She attempted a compromise by eating whole wheat pancakes with real maple syrup and health-food margarine, but it did not fulfill her. Only Aunt Jemima's pancakes with artificial syrup and cholesterol-laden butter could do the trick. Her question was this: Should she give in to her craving because it felt so good even though it went against her diet and her nutritional beliefs, or should she avoid it, yet feel as though she was cheating herself out of a deeply satisfying experience? This is one of the fascinating areas in eating where the distinctions between good nutrition and good nourishment are blurred. The answer is simply a matter of personal choice because we can make either strategy work.

## When Cravings Clash with Beliefs

Vegetarians often remark that after a number of months or years on their diet they begin craving meat or fish. This causes great conflict because their body is saying one thing but their dietary beliefs clearly say something else. Followers of a macrobiotic diet experience similar conflict with dairy products, which are seen as unhealthy according to macrobiotic principles. Compounding the confusion is the oft-stated concept that the vegetarian's craving for meat is merely an outdated desire temporarily resurfacing, or the macrobiotic dieter's craving for dairy products is an unhealthy impulse trying to "cleanse" its way out of the body. These theories are probably true in some instances, but who can say for sure when they apply and when they do not. The important point is that the more we crave a food not in our nutritional belief system and the more we hold to the belief that the food is bad, the less open we will be to assess the true nature of the situation.

A woman I met had followed a vegetarian diet for seven years and was suddenly craving meat. She was distraught and felt like a criminal for having such impulses. Worse still, her health mysteriously began to fail and she was quite under-weight. For months she fantasized about eating steak but would not allow herself to do it. Her body was filled with the desire, but her mind was in turmoil about what this meant. She finally broke down, had a steak, enjoyed it, and watched her health improve as she began to include each week several meat dishes in her diet. She uncovered the true nature of her desire through direct bodily experience, not by arguing belief systems. I am not suggesting that vegetarians should eat meat. I am simply suggesting that the same nutritional beliefs that have helped us can also limit us when we forget the changing nature of body and diet.

## Somatic Anchoring

Longing to be with someone has a complex biochemical expression in the body—a series of neurological, hormonal, electrochemical, and motor responses that give us the physio-logical sensation of longing. Likewise, longing for food is somatically anchored in the body. Each craving has its own biochemical milieu, a network of reactions that encode in the body.

For example, if we ate chocolate chip cookies every day at lunch for several months, the body's biocomputer would pro-gram itself for this event. All the sensory input and digestive responses involved in eating chocolate chip cookies at noon would be habituated in the body. Should the cookies fail to appear, the body would miss them.

Originally the cookies appealed to our taste and captured our imagination. Over time the body, too, is "captured." It must have the experience it is habituated to. This form of dependency is similar to zoo animals that grow restless when the zookeeper is late with daily meals, when people are anxious because the pizza at their favorite pizza place isn't as good as usual that day, or when a drug addict goes through withdrawal when a fix is unavailable.

My craving for bran muffins and ice cream was somatically anchored and expressed itself when the absence of these foods was felt. The craving originally took hold because three important conditions were met: (1) I ate bran muffins and ice cream every day for several months; (2) My emotional need grew stronger and stronger; (3) The foods themselves were more concentrated and potent relative to other foods. That is, just as certain drugs are more powerful and addictive than others, so are certain foods more powerful and potentially addictive. These three conditions—frequency of intake, intensity of psychological need, and potency of substance—are found in a majority of dispersive cravings.

Because the experience of any food we have eaten with great frequency is held in our central nervous system in much the same way as a computer stores information, certain stimuli (e.g., pushing the right key) will access the neural patterning for that particular food and cause it to be fired. For example, in an associative craving the stimulus of seeing our parents may activate the circuitry for foods associated with our childhood. It is akin to a drug "flashback," a biological trigger that when pressed momentarily returns us to a past experience.

Every negative habit and every dispersive craving has a

similar neurological triggering process. When confronted with certain stimuli, particularly negative or painful ones, we are automatically drawn to substances that we associate with alleviating the pain and providing us immediate pleasure: alcohol, sugar, et cetera. This is why cravings and habits are so difficult to deal with. They are encoded in the body and are activated without conscious input. The key to transforming a craving is to introduce an effective *conscious* intervention. And this is where the "holding technique" proves to be the simplest and most successful method.

## The Holding Technique

The holding technique is a method that allows us to move through a craving without yielding to it. It helps release the locked-in tension that intensifies a craving, and practiced over time it repatterns neural messages so that the craving is no longer anchored in the body, and our dependency on the food disappears.

I did not know it then, but I was practicing this technique on the couch resisting the bran muffins and vanilla ice cream. The method is simply this: Breathe through a craving, fully experience all the sensations that arise, allow emotions to be fully expressed, and arrive at the place where you no longer need yield to the desire.

The holding technique is understood in many different disciplines and known by different names. Runners know it as the "second wind." When a runner feels tired, lethargic, cramped, or in pain, when all impulses say "stop," yet the runner continues to run and breathe through these hindering forces, a breakthrough occurs. The pain vanishes, the second wind appears, and a powerful energy is released. Yoga practitioners use this technique by literally holding still in a difficult yoga posture, bringing the body to the edge between tension and comfort, and then experiencing the pain, the *fear* of the pain, and simply witnessing any thoughts of giving up while continuing to maintain the posture. In time, the pain vanishes, the body moves even more deeply into the posture, and a great sense of pleasure and freedom is experienced.

The holding technique is not limited to athletes. Artists, musicians, writers, and those involved in other creative or business pursuits understand the process of persevering during "dry," difficult, and painful periods and eventually seeing the light at the end of the tunnel, a burst of new energy or creative insight. In fact, the holding technique applies to any difficulty faced in life. It is based on the principle that given time, pain and fear will pass.

As I was sitting there on the couch, experiencing the sensations and emotions that were surfacing in response to my bran-muffins-and-ice-cream craving, I eventually tapped into a deeper source of pain and longing of which the craving was only a small part. By releasing the pain, I released the desire that went along with it. I got my second wind, a feeling of renewed energy and deep relaxation.

The next time you feel an urge or a craving for something you know does not serve you, a desire you would like to transform, try the simple steps of the holding technique. Sit somewhere comfortable, breathe full deep breaths, and see what happens if you wait till the urge passes. It is important to witness all the feelings and physical sensations that arise without suppressing and fighting them. Experience them but don't cater to them.

When a craving arises or when we are confronted with any difficult emotional experience, a part of us believes that the pain will last forever. We *do* survive and the pain does subside. Yet the next time a similar situation occurs we forget again and believe our discomfort to be eternal. The key is to trust that with patience and compassion the pain will pass.

In such instances we generally have a "first reaction," an immediate response that it is best not to act on. For example, if we are angered by someone, we might want to retaliate by hitting or saying something we might regret later on. If we crave sugar, we might want to reach for a piece of cake. The purpose of the holding technique is to let the first reaction pass so that we can see what lies beyond it.

The technique is not a one-shot deal that eliminates a craving or pain every time. The bran-muffin-and-ice-cream incident was an extreme example. Yet little breakthroughs can be made each time you allow yourself to breathe through a craving or any difficult situation. All one need do, all one can do, is witness, experience, and accept.

## KEY LESSONS

- There are three general types of cravings: supportive cravings that help the body, dispersive cravings that harm it, and associative cravings that arise from deep-seated memories.

- We often crave foods that clash with our nutritional beliefs. The more we hold an idea that a food we crave is bad, the less open we are to assess the true nature of our craving.

- When we are uncertain about the nature of a craving, experimentation and direct bodily experience provide the most useful insights.

- Dispersive cravings are encoded in our nervous system and are activated automatically. By consciously intervening in this process, a craving can be released.

## REFLECTIONS

- Can you recall instances when you craved a food, ate it, and experienced a positive or healing effect in your body? Was the food something you knew would be good for you, or did it seem like an unusual craving?

- Can you recall an instance of craving a food, eating it, and feeling negative reactions in the body? What symptoms appeared that convinced you the craving was an unhealthy one? If you knew it would not benefit you, yet you ate it anyway, what was it that made you override your own understanding?

- Do you ever crave foods associated with your childhood or any other part of your past? What activates these cravings? How do you respond to them? How does it feel to fulfill them?

- Choose a memorable food you ate during childhood but have not eaten since, and eat it. Observe the thoughts and feelings that emerge.

- Have you ever craved a food considered taboo in your dietary philosophy? Did this cause confusion? How did you resolve the conflict? What did you learn?

- Choose a favorite or staple food that you eat every day (or almost every day) and don't eat it for a week. Note any physical or emotional reactions.

- Interview friends, relatives, or coworkers who drink coffee or eat sugar every day. Ask them if they have ever tried to stop or if they want to stop. Compare the results.

- Are there any instances in life when you have naturally used the holding technique (moving through your pain to reach a second wind)? What did the experience teach you? How can you apply it to the rest of your life?

# 11

## Whole Body Eating

During a particularly stressful time in my life I was looking for the right vacation spot to help me unwind and feel more relaxed about life. A friend had recently returned from a ten-day meditation retreat in the country and was clearly a changed man. He explained that from four-thirty in the morning till nine in the evening, all the participants did was sit in silence and meditate. There were short breaks for meals, walks, and the bathroom. Otherwise, it was pure silence for ten days. No socializing, no talking, no music, no videos, and no external distractions. It helped him calm down and gave him a very positive outlook on life. He suggested I give it a try. It sounded like the last situation I would put myself in, but a few weeks later I decided to try it.

After the initial "excitement" of meditating eleven hours a day wore off, there was not much to look forward to when waking up each morning. Because all possible distractions and diversions were eliminated, there was only one thing to grab onto—food. Each day 160 meditators eagerly waited for the breakfast, lunch, and dinner bells to ring. Once in the dining hall, people would pile their plates with a surprisingly large amount of food. It was certainly not because they were exercising all day and needed more calories than usual. It was because the process of meditation can bring up boredom, anxiety, tension, and a host of negative emotions, and food was the only available source of immediate gratification. Many people would eat so much so fast that they would fall asleep during the meditation session. Here they were attempting to observe and "control" their minds during eleven hours of meditation each day, yet at mealtimes they ate recklessly, shoveling down their food with little attention.

I was observing the way everyone else ate and noting the extent of their emotional eating, but by about the fourth day I realized that I was behaving no differently. Not only was I using food as an emotional crutch, eating in an unconscious trance without any awareness of my food, I realized that I always ate that way. I could not remember ever eating with a quiet mind, focusing attention on my food, and really tasting the full experience of eating.

This insight swept over me just as I was about to take my first bite of lunch, and the impact of this *aha* experience sent me into uncontrollable laughter. There I was, sitting in the dining hall with 160 meditators who had been silent for four days, and I was laughing at the top of my lungs, unable to stop myself. When I finally took a bite of my food, it felt like the first bite in the universe. I now knew what it meant to "savor" food, to experience whole body eating.

Once I had swallowed that first blissful mouthful, I again broke into uncontrollable belly laughs. In these moments of laughing and eating, I was enlightened. Others around me seemed desperate to merge with God. I had merged with food! Needless to say, I attracted quite a bit of attention. I had not noticed it before, but everyone was transfixed by my performance. Two concerned and serious "monitors" were summoned, and they inquired if I was presently on drugs. I explained that all I had done was eat, and that it had sent me into ecstasy. They eyed me suspiciously, whispered a few words to each other, and told me that if I wanted to be in ecstasy, I would have to do it quietly.

I have found that the best things in life are not only free but also simple. We often look for intricate ways to fix ourselves, and in doing so miss the obvious. Awareness cures. Giving attention to eating is the most fundamental level of healing we can reach in our relationship to food. It is also the most rewarding. Experiencing the body brings unimaginable joy and satisfaction, sometimes quiet and subdued, at other times ecstatic and uninhibited. If you eat, you owe it to yourself to experience what you eat. "Whole body eating" is a simple practice of eating with awareness that can be done each day with minimal effort and maximal results. It is a step-by-step process that includes five of the most basic and powerful eating habits one can practice. It can be used with any type of diet or any problems you may experience with food.

As we have seen, negative habits are mechanical. We may understand exactly what is good for us and know how to eat, yet there is no guarantee we will do what is right. This is the paradoxical nature of the mind: Knowing does not lead to doing. Negative habits are so mechanical that we are compelled to repeat them even when we want to stop. Practicing the positive habits of whole body eating helps us starve the negative ones. Remember: It is not necessary to fight an unwanted habit to eliminate it. Cultivate the habits that truly nurture you, and the negative ones will simply wither and die. Whole body eating is especially effective because it helps bypass our mental traps and brings us back to one of the most important sources of transformation—the body.

The body is a superior source of nutritional information for one simple reason: It does not lie. It reports information and reports it accurately. If our body has a broken arm, we feel pain; if our body is in a peak experience of pleasure, we feel ecstasy; when our body is exhausted from exercise, we feel tired; when our body is hungry, it tells us to eat. And as we have seen, when the body is fulfilled, it won't tell us to eat, but the mind may. The body reports its sensations, but the mind may respond through its habits and conditioning.

Characteristically the body has one common response to the mind's destructive habits: numbness. When the mind continually commands the body to act against the body's wisdom, the body desensitizes itself to the fundamental biological messages that inform us about our well-being. For example, when the mind commands the body to overeat, the body numbs itself to the physiological sensations of fullness or satisfaction, and we continue to eat past the point of nutritional need.

In medical terminology this numbness is called *tolerance.* The body can build up a tolerance to drugs, alcohol, and even food. Many people need three or four cups of coffee to get the effects of one, while others can consume a six-pack of beer with little effect. And as every "tolerant" person knows, the moment we pass our point of tolerance, something inside us changes radically. This is why people with dangerously unhealthy habits can stay healthy for years, and suddenly fall seriously ill. They never had a clue to their declining health because the body was desensitized to the fundamental messages that arise naturally, moment to moment. One of my favorite comics depicts a man who has finally come into the doctor's office for a checkup. He no longer looks like a human being but like an amorphous blob of jelly melted over the chair with two eyes sticking out and a hat somewhere on top. The doctor sitting behind the desk politely says to him, "Mr. Smith, I think you've been lacking calcium in your diet."

Instead of waiting for a health crisis to force us to pay attention to the body, cultivate body wisdom now and learn to work with the body as it changes from day to day. Whole body eating is particularly useful for those of us who love to say, "I know what's wrong with me. I know what my problem is. I know what I need to do. *I just don't do it!*" As you've probably realized by now, nothing happens until you do something. The five steps give you something to do that yields results. Allow yourself to practice these exercises for even one week, and your relationship to food will be transformed. You will also notice the changes echoing in everything else you do.

## THE FIVE STEPS OF WHOLE BODY EATING

*Step 1:* Make a conscious choice to eat.

*Step 2:* Ask your body what it wants.

*Step 3:* Eat with awareness.

*Step 4:* Listen for feedback.

*Step 5:* Release the meal.

**STEP 1:** *Make a Conscious Choice to Eat.*

Chances are good that you eat at least three times a day with some snacking in between. How often, though, do you question yourself to see if eating is what you really want to do?

Many of us eat on automatic pilot. We are driven by habit

to eat when we are not hungry or not to eat when we are hungry. In the first step of whole body eating we perform the most basic act of the eating process. We look within to see what we are hungering for. We make the conscious choice of whether or not to eat.

### Exercise

Before you put anything in your mouth, ask yourself:

Am I hungry?
Will food satisfy my hunger?
What would truly nourish me in this moment?
Do I choose to eat?

Once you have asked these questions, make the choice. And remember: whatever choice you make, accept it fully. The act of consciously examining the decision to eat may produce conflict. You will see your blind spots and weaknesses. Rather than judge these as faults, simply be aware of them. If you choose to eat, eat without resistance and punishment.

I am not advocating reckless eating. I am recommending responsibility through conscious choice. I am suggesting gentle self-acceptance as a way to diffuse the charge you build up around food. As you practice this awareness technique, the choice becomes easier and clearer.

Use Step 1 of whole body eating whenever you feel hungry—it takes only a minute. By making a conscious decision to eat, you may feel as if you are claiming your body as your own for the first time. Can you think of a better person to be in charge?

**STEP 2:** *Ask Your Body What It Wants.*

Once you have decided to eat, consciously choose *what* to eat. In fact, go to an authority for advice: your body. The body has an intuitive wisdom that goes beyond words and explanations. Dancers, healers, yogis, athletes, and others know this. You know it too: You just may not know that you know it.

**Exercise**

Before you reach for any food, sit down, close your eyes, take a deep breath, and let yourself be empty of expectations. With a quiet relaxed mind, ask your body what it hungers for, and ask it to be specific. Allow yourself to connect to the body's intuitive wisdom, the part of you that naturally knows the foods which would best nourish.

You may be surprised at the answers that come, or you may feel as if the answers are "just right." If there's any doubt in your mind, simply allow the doubt to be there. Trust that by experimenting in this way, you are entering into a learning process where you will make a few mistakes and enjoy a few successes.

Through practicing this exercise, we begin to experience the dynamic and changing nature of the body. From day to day and season to season, the body changes in size, metabolism, energy needs. And at any given time the body beckons for a different kind of food.

When I ask my body what to eat, the answers I get invariably *work*. During the cold winter months my body naturally reaches for more cooked foods and warm soups. In the summer months it desires more fruits and liquids. At times of emotional stress, my appetite decreases and my body "breaks down" in weight. During times of abundance and great self-confidence I can eat twice as much food and not gain an ounce. Some weeks I am attracted to eating cooked greens. Other weeks I am drawn to anything red: beets, plums, cherries, red peppers. When autumn comes I long for squash. When I am low on energy or think I am getting sick, I automatically reach for ginger. The list goes on.

Many of us mistrust the body. We believe that if we let our body do what it wants to do, it will go wild and eat fudge bars and frozen yogurt all day. Yet it is not really the body we fear. We mistrust the mind and what we think the mind will do to the body. The key here is to move beyond fear to a place where we are willing to experiment.

If you are concerned about asking your body and getting the "wrong" answers, remember that choosing the "right" foods is less important than eating whatever you choose *wholeheartedly*. We eat what we eat regardless of whether we tune into our body wisdom or not, so why not just enjoy it. It is perfectly fine to draw on somatic information and make mistakes. The more we practice the better we become.

**STEP 3:** *Eat with Awareness.*

This is the heart of whole body eating: Be there when you eat. Achieve the fullest experience of your food. Taste it. Savor it. Pay attention to it. Rejoice in it. See how it makes your body feel. Take in all the sensations.

But don't just eat the food. Eat the ambiance. Eat the colors. Eat the aromas. Eat the conversation. Eat the company sitting next to you. Eat the entire experience.

Have you ever really eaten? Many of us haven't had a "pure" experience of food. We eat but are "out to lunch." We are busy with something else or drifting off in fantasyland. This fundamental inattention to the meal leaves us starving for more. We may eat a nutritionally complete meal yet still remain undernourished.

We don't just hunger for food alone. We hunger for the experience of it—the tasting, the chewing, the sensuousness, the enjoyment, the textures, the sounds, and the satisfaction. If we continually miss these experiences, we will naturally want to eat again and again, but will remain unfulfilled.

**Exercise**

Find a time when you feel unhurried and can put your obligations aside. Be alone. Cook yourself a meal that you will enjoy eating. Then take the food to a comfortable room where you can be undistracted. Sit with your back straight. Let your eyes close. Take three or four deep breaths. When you are relaxed, allow your eyes to open and look at your food. Sense your hunger for it. Smell it. Wonder about it. And then eat it.

Notice all the sensations in your body. Feel the food in your mouth and on your tongue. Listen to the sounds of chewing. Follow the food as it goes down your throat. At what point does it disappear from your awareness? Can you feel the moment-to-moment changes from excitement to relaxation to anticipation as you consume your meal? Eat slowly and deliberately. Do nothing else for twenty minutes but immerse yourself in eating. Don't go off to Jupiter, become president of the United States, or digest more newsprint than food. No distractions of any kind. Issues and emotions are bound to emerge as you eat— fear, excitement, longing, confusion, boredom. As you watch these come up, allow them to go by. Return to the food. Surrender yourself to a 100-percent experience of eating.

People who practice this experiment often report that they feel as if they are tasting food for the first time. One woman could not believe she had spent a whole lifetime without noticing her food. Eating with awareness helps us use the bodily sensations experienced during a meal as an anchor for the restless mind, a mind that can't wait to eat yet refuses to pay attention once it *is* eating. When we are relaxed, receptive, attentive, and without self-rejection, doubt, expectations, or judgments, we are in the most appropriate condition for the digestive system to function at its optimal level.

If we eat in a stressful state, the digestive system functions less efficiently and may even shut down. The sympathetic nervous system is activated and the digestive process is automatically suppressed. Enzymatic output of the stomach, pancreas, and small intestines is inhibited while the amount of blood flow to the digestive system is decreased. This quick shutdown is commonly experienced as heartburn, stomach pains, intestinal gas, nausea, or general sensations of dullness and heaviness. It is not only the food that creates digestive distress, but also the emotional state of the eater.

Eating with awareness increases the nutrient assimilation of a meal as well as the assimilation of the entire sensory experience. Obviously you cannot eat this way all the time, but you can incorporate the essence of "conscious eating" into any eating situation. Try devoting at least a few minutes of each meal to conscious eating. You may also wish to set aside several meals during the week for conscious, silent dining.

If your mind wanders or your mental state is unsatisfactory during a meal, allow yourself simply to witness this and accept it. Even if you want to eat *without* awareness—bingeing, swallowing food whole, reading, watching TV, or "pigging out"— at least be aware that you are choosing to be unaware and don't criticize yourself for doing so. As a Zen master once observed about the importance of doing anything whole-heartedly, "When I'm there, I'm totally there. When I'm not there, I'm totally not there."

Eating with awareness is the most important and powerful tool to transform your relationship to food and the body. Once you begin to practice it, it becomes a lifelong habit. There is no goal or ideal to strive for. All there is to do is eat, observe, and accept. No matter what kind of food you eat or nutritional system you follow, eating with awareness is the key to diet.

**STEP 4:** *Listen for Feedback.*

Now that you have eaten your meal, take a few minutes to relax. Learn from the meal by reflecting upon *what* you have eaten and *how* you have eaten it. You have already fed the body. Complete the circle by letting it feed you—feedback.

**Exercise**

Sit down quietly after your meal. Take five to ten slow, deep breaths. Then listen carefully to your body. Did you pay attention to the meal? Did the food satisfy you? Would you eat differently next time? Slower, faster? Consume more food, less food, different food? Did you overeat? Do you feel heavy? Are you still hungry? What would make your meal complete?

Experience the sensation of having food in your body. Can you feel the effects of your meal in any particular places—stomach, intestines, throat, eyes, sinuses, tongue, teeth? You may have a warm, satisfied feeling. You may feel anxious or sluggish. Do you recall any of the thoughts or emotions you experienced during the meal? Can you draw any connections between the "ingredients" of your meal and the way you are feeling?

Take whatever information that comes to you and simply note it. If you are unhappy with how you feel or how you have eaten, try not to punish yourself. Relax. Use the experience as a teacher, as a method to improve the way you eat next time.

This step will enable you to learn which foods work best for you and which eating patterns work against you. Listening for feedback not only provides information immediately after eating but is also useful for several hours or even several days after a meal. Often the effects of a meal are not apparent until later on. The challenge is to learn how to recognize connections between what we feel now and what we ate then.

Look for the clues your body offers to help determine the effectiveness of a meal. Each of us has a unique way in which we react to a meal. Some may experience a sinus reaction to a particular food; some feel it in the throat, eyes, tongue, or chest. I have noticed that soda consistently makes my teeth hurt and dulls the sensation on my tongue, anything fried or greasy gives me pimples two days later, potatoes make me feel sluggish, and red wine gives me a headache.

I don't label these foods bad and I don't make their existence a crime against humanity. I just don't eat them because I don't enjoy the sensations they produce. Even if I eat something that I know is unhealthy for me, I do not punish myself. I am simply aware of it and learn from it. Self-acceptance is the key. Accept yourself no matter how you eat, and you lay the groundwork for real and lasting change.

**STEP 5:** *Release the Meal.*

Once you have finished your food, let it go. Forget about eating for a while. Forget about health, weight, and anything that looks, smells, or tastes like food. Go on to the next thing at hand. Live your life. Be free. Do any of the million wonderful things you can do that have nothing to do with food.

This is the last step in whole body eating and perhaps the most difficult. The inability to release food is at the root of our most challenging eating habits. Even though we have finished a meal, the eating has not really ended. The mind may continue to munch on thoughts of food, dieting, body image, or optimum nutrition. Do you realize the tremendous amount of energy spent by holding on to these things? Do you see how self-expression can be stifled by excessive worries and concerns about food?

People with difficulty releasing food often find themselves bored and unengaged after a meal. They may be stuck in the house, alone in an unfamiliar setting, or unable to find anything meaningful to do. Under these conditions the mind naturally gravitates back to food. Some people bind themselves to food the instant the meal is finished. They think about food, talk about it, work around it (in the kitchen or on the job), or socialize with food-obsessed friends. Though they sincerely yearn to let go of food, everything they do after a meal conspires to bring them back to eating. Releasing food can be as natural and spontaneous as eating it. It can also be as satisfying. Know that you *can* release food. And with that release comes a freedom to direct your energy as you choose.

**Exercise**

Consciously practice releasing food when your meal is over. Ask yourself, What's next? and go on to a new activity. The more wholeheartedly you do whatever comes next, the less the mind will wander back to food. If you have free time and lack structured activities after a meal, ask yourself, What would engage me fully in this moment? What can I do that is useful and enjoyable?

Avoid a continuous munch session after the meal is over. Shift the conversation away from food and diet. Observe the little things you do that prevent you from release and gently drop them. No one is holding on but you. You won't fall if you let go. You'll fly.

Perhaps the biggest obstacle to releasing food is our inability to "assimilate" it. Many of us finish a meal without any integration time. We eat and run, fall asleep from overeating, or become a couch vegetable (common varieties include potato, squash, and sprout). The experience of eating remains undigested like morsels of food in an upset stomach.

Once you have listened for feedback about the meal, take time to just be with it. Celebrate. Listen to music, talk to friends, stare out the window, read a book, or just breathe. There is more to celebration than just enjoying yourself. At a deeper level it represents not only the acknowledgment of change but also in some way the act of assimilation. Nutrients are absorbed at the cellular level, and an exchange goes on at the social level. Have you noticed how people often become reflective after a meal, how crying babies become happy, how couples "open up" to each other, and how relatives at a holiday dinner become a little less obnoxious?

You are a new person after you have eaten.

Introduce yourself.

### KEY LESSONS

- The ongoing practice of positive habits helps transform our relationship to food.

- There are five key steps in making our relationship to food more conscious. They are:

1. Consciously choosing whether or not to eat.
2. Tuning in to the body to help determine its needs.
3. Eating with awareness of the entire experience.
4. Listening to the body for feedback after the meal.
5. Releasing thoughts of food when the meal is finished and moving on to the next thing.

## REFLECTIONS

- How much of your eating is automatic and without thought as to whether or not you are truly hungry?

- Can you recall any instances when you felt particularly attuned to your body's needs? What were the sensations that helped you understand what your body wanted? What would help you remain attuned in this way?

- How often do you eat with awareness of your meal? What are the benefits of eating with awareness? What would help you focus more on your food?

- Do you ever observe the effects of a meal you have eaten? Do you consistently have certain physical reactions or symptoms when you eat? What do you think causes these reactions?

- How often do you think or fantasize about food? Why do you think so many people are preoccupied with eating?

- As an experiment, go on a fast for one day. Drink lots of water, but try not to eat any food. Observe your physical state and note the thoughts about eating that come up throughout the day.

- Find a special eating bowl or plate just for you, one that really catches your eye and inspires you to eat from it. Use it for all your meals for a week and note any changes in your experience of eating.

- Think of an item in which you demand quality and integrity (car, stereo system, music, furniture, clothing). Then imagine what would happen if you translated that same demand for quality to the food you eat.

# 12

# *Natural Alignment*

Have you ever considered your body posture while eating? Can the position of your body influence your experience of a meal? Can it affect digestive capacity and nutritional assimilation? Perhaps you have already noticed how many people slouch or hunch over when they eat. Do you have any idea of the remarkable series of abnormal biological events that this causes?

When the head is bent, the tongue is tipped forward and down. This means that most of the food that enters the mouth touches the front portion of the tongue only. The less the food is exposed to the full surface of the tongue, the fewer signals are sent to the brain and the less we taste. Different parts of the tongue have different degrees of sensitivity to the four basic tastes: sweet, salty, sour, and bitter. By allowing only one part of the tongue to sense the food, the complex chemical and neural pathways that interact to produce taste are diminished. So not only do we taste less, but the sensations we do receive are only partial.

When the neck and upper body are tilted forward the esophagus is constricted. This muscular tube normally contracts and relaxes with waves of motion called peristalsis that causes food to move to the stomach. If we slouch, the peristaltic waves occur irregularly and may even "lock" the food in one place. This is what happens when we say something is "sticking in our throat."

In addition, slouching makes it difficult for the soft palate (upperback portion of the mouth) to close off the nasopharynx (entranceway to nasal passages). Food may then go up instead of down. This is the cause of the nasal congestion many slouchy eaters experience and is the reason why the food or liquid we consume sometimes "comes out of our nose."

The slouched position also inhibits respiration. The trachea (windpipe), which rests in front of the esophagus, becomes pinched, so less air reaches the lungs. In the body's natural response to oxygenate fully, the epiglottis, which normally closes off the passageway to the trachea when food is ingested, will sporadically open at the wrong time. Morsels of food will then sneak down the trachea instead of the esophagus. This is what happens when we say, "Food went down the wrong pipe." Equally important, decreased oxygenation during slouching also means decreased metabolic capacity for digestion. The biochemical reactions in the digestive system depend on full, healthy respiration. Less oxygen means less digestive fire.

Furthermore, a slouched body means a scrunched midsection. The anatomical positions normally occupied by the digestive organs (stomach, liver, gall bladder, intestines, pancreas) are disturbed. The organs push against each other in an unnatural fashion, causing decreased blood flow and diminished digestive function.

Finally, with the cervical and thoracic vertebrae of the spinal cord bent over, spinal nerves are compressed. Though any of the spinal nerves can be affected depending upon the location of the spinal flexion, the net effect is always decreased nervous activity to the brain. Research reveals that the angle of the spine while sitting significantly influences our ability to retain information and think logically. The greater the curvature of the spine, the less the ability to process information in all three major divisions of the brain. Dancers, martial artists, and gymnasts all understand the profound effect a properly aligned spinal column has on alertness and performance. Because overall function of the brain is diminished during slouchy eating, the result is any combination of decreased function in taste sensation, respiration, digestive capacity, awareness of appetite, and conscious awareness of the meal.

Natural alignment of the body is a precursor to fullness of experience not only on the biological level, but also on the psychological level. The subjective experience of eating is dramatically different when you bring food to you rather than bring yourself to it (slouching). Eating with the back straight, chin parallel to the earth, shoulders relaxed, and knees slightly lower than the hips instills a psychological poise. We create a sense of dignity, watchfulness, and quiet self-respect. We distinguish ourselves as "human."

A businessman I met at a health conference had complained of chronic gas and indigestion for many years. He had consulted many doctors and digestive specialists and nothing helped. I was intrigued by his vast knowledge of nutrition and his determined search to cure his condition. That evening I spotted him in the dining hall. As I made my way toward his table, I stopped halfway—shocked. He was as hunched over the table as possible without actually lying on top of his food. His face was directed straight down, and he resembled a puppy dog lapping up food.

He finished his meal, straightened his body, and after a hurried greeting he started to discourse on his new diet to alleviate indigestion. I suggested gently that a different body posture while eating might resolve his problem, and I outlined some of my ideas. He seemed unimpressed but agreed to give it a try. Several months later he sent me a letter. His gas problem, indigestion, and congested sinuses had cleared significantly simply by changing the position of his body.

As an experiment, eat something in a slouched position. Bend your back, lower your head, and notice the taste of the food. What happens when it touches the tongue, your breathing pattern, and the general experience of eating this way. Does slouching produce a particular mental-emotional state?

Next, sit upright with the chin horizontal to the floor, shoulders relaxed, and back straight. Bring the food *to* you. Notice the difference in taste, the way the food moves in your mouth and down your throat, your breathing, and your awareness of the meal. Is your mental state different in an upright posture? Can you feel the advantages of eating in an aligned position? Are there other areas in life where more attention to body posture would be of benefit?

## KEY LESSONS

- Body posture affects every sensory experience.

- The position of the body while eating profoundly affects digestion and nutrient assimilation.

- It also significantly influences our experience of ourselves and the meal.

## REFLECTIONS

- Are you generally conscious of body posture while eating? How do you usually sit?

- As you read this, lean forward, round your back, and dip your head down. Observe your mental experience of reading while slouching. Now sit up straight, hold the book in front of you at eye level, and feel the difference.

- Observe the eating posture of people you know. Judging by their posture, what would your initial impression of them be if you did not know them?

- Observe the posture of patrons in a restaurant. What can you learn about them from how they sit?

- While dining with others, begin eating from a dignified, upright position. Then gradually bend forward until you are eating from the most slouched position possible. Observe other people's reactions.

# 13

# The Psychobiology of Chewing

Have you ever wondered why crunchy foods are so popular, why advertisers promote products on the basis of crunchiness—"super-crunchy," "extra crunchy," "stays crunchy even in milk"? Have you noticed that whenever you eat your favorite brand of potato chips, pretzels, or crackers, it always has the same level of crunchiness? What advertisers understand and capitalize on is that crunching and chewing are primal activities, inborn urges dating back to the first life-forms that ever "crunched" each other.

So important is the level of crunch that potato-chip manufacturers developed a sophisticated apparatus to measure the perceived level of crunch that test subjects heard in their heads. The most pleasurable decibel levels were recorded, and potato chips were then manufactured to these standard crunch levels.

Chewing and crunching are organic outlets for inborn aggression. Throw a piece of meat into a lion's cage and the lion will roar at it, attack it, and tear it apart as if it were still alive. The lion must do this because it is its nature to be aggressive. Aggression here is not meant as some mean, vengeful act. A lion does not attack a jackrabbit because of hate. Quite the contrary, the lion attacks because it *loves* jackrabbit.

Like the lion, human beings have a distinct measure of innate aggression, and this aggression is first experienced through the bite. Psychologists talk about the original oral-aggressive act as the "hanging-on bite" to the breast. This is a biting that establishes confluence with the mother. The baby must actively hold on for nourishment and will often keep holding on even when the mother has had enough. The tension it experiences when separated from the mother before it is fully satisfied is then expressed through crying, screaming, and facial contortions.

In the various body-oriented disciplines (Reich, Alexander, Feldenkrais, et al.), the jaw is associated with anger and aggression. When these emotions are habitually withheld and left unexpressed, they may become "frozen" on the face as a perpetually clenched jaw and tightened musculature resembling a scowl. Just as a dog clenches its teeth when angered or challenged, so human beings channel aggression through the face. From an evolutionary perspective the process of biting and chewing allows for the release of what psychologists call dental aggression. The pleasure and satisfaction that come from eating crunchy foods result from a decrease in tension that has built up within the body. In other words, chewing and crunching naturally help fulfill our primal aggressive urges.

Many people habitually fail to chew, swallowing food almost whole. They tend to derive pleasure not so much from the taste and chewing of food as from the velocity at which it is eaten. In such instances we deny an important natural outlet for aggression and fail to experience full satisfaction from a meal. In an effort to free the unreleased tension, we may continue to eat past the point of satiation, turn to other oral-based habits, or simply internalize the tension, allowing it to build over time and eventually express itself in chronic emotional or biological symptoms.

On another level, by swallowing food whole, we make a statement about the way we approach the world. We want our hungers in life satisfied but are unwilling to take the necessary steps. This need for immediate gratification is reflected in our refusal to chew. Ironically, a side effect of the short-cut method of not chewing is more hunger. Chewing and tasting are basic to hunger satisfaction. We may claim to enjoy eating yet fail to notice what is in our mouth.

In one fascinating experiment scientists deprived a group of test rats of taste sensation. Both this group and a control group were placed on normal rat diets, and in a short time the taste-deprived rats all died. When the rats were autopsied, scientists could find only one cause of death—clinical malnutrition. The scientists could come up with only one explanation—that there are important yet unknown physiological connections between taste and health. Similarly, hospital patients fed intravenously or through feeding tubes that bypass the mouth often report a nagging hunger for taste. Though the mechanisms that govern these phenomena are little understood, this much is certain: To be fully nourished by food, we must experience it through tasting and chewing.

In a comparable manner, to be fully nourished by *any* experience, we must "taste" and "chew" it thoroughly. It is no accident that the words we use to describe eating are the same words used to describe the thinking process. When presented with an idea, the mind will first grasp it and "chew" on it. Our conscious mind breaks it down into its component parts, "tastes" it, then "swallows" it into the subconscious for final "assimilation." When we accept something without "ruminating" over it or when we swallow something "hook, line, and sinker," or when "biting off more than we can chew," what we say in metaphoric language is that just as food works with digestion, so do perceptions work with the mind. Improper chewing of food or ideas are equally disturbing to our system.

The mouth is the first step in the digestive process. Here the chemical digestion of starches is initiated with amylase, an enzyme that breaks down the complex carbohydrate molecules in a well-salivated mouth. The *mechanical* digestion of food is also initiated in the mouth with the process of chewing. The surface area increases as the food is broken down into smaller and smaller pieces. When the food reaches the stomach, the number of molecules exposed to the stomach's acid and enzymatic environment is maximized.

If we swallow something whole, such as a piece of meat, an abnormal series of events occurs. First the stomach must churn the meat with its own muscular movements to help break it down into smaller pieces, a function it is not really designed to do. Next, we go through the lengthy chemical process of breaking down large pieces of food. Because we started with one large bite, only the surface of the meat remains exposed to the stomach's digestive juices. To digest the meat further, the stomach may secrete more acid than normal. This irritates the stomach lining, which is the reason many eaters experience acid indigestion. The condition is exacerbated if the food is high in protein. The greater the protein content of a food, the higher the level of stomach acidity required to digest it.

Furthermore, we are often in a stressful state and pressured for time and therefore do not chew. Stress itself can cause excess acid production. Couple this with large pieces of unchewed food in the stomach, and we help create ideal conditions for stomach acid to digest the stomach lining—ulcers.

Chewing is a "pacesetter." Whatever speed and number of times we chew sets in motion a rhythm that our entire body adopts. By chewing rapidly and insufficiently, we initiate an unsettled frame of mind that is reflected in the body as uncomfortable sensations in the digestive system. Chewing at a moderate to slow rate promotes a relaxed, grounded demeanor and for many a noticeably stronger metabolism.

Full chewing need not be a discipline but can occur spontaneously simply by eating with relaxed awareness. Rather than concentrate on chewing food, *eat* your food, and let chewing be a natural part of the eating process.

## KEY LESSONS

- Chewing and crunching are natural outlets for aggression.

- The way we chew food is a metaphor for the way we notice and discriminate with our mind.

- Chewing affects digestion and the assimilation of nutrients.

- The way we chew affects our mood and our subjective experience of eating.

- Chewing is a learned process.

## REFLECTIONS

- Do you chew your food? Do you *know* if you chew your food?

- Do you enjoy crunchy foods? What do you experience while crunching? What part of you does it satisfy?

- Why do people eat popcorn at the movies?

- Observe how dogs, cats, and domesticated birds chew their food. Can they teach you anything? Can you teach them anything?

- Why is taste so important? Why does taste differ from person to person? What do you think would happen if for one week you could not eat any foods with appealing taste? What would happen if you lost your ability to taste?

- For one day give attention to chewing. Simply observe the way you chew without trying to change anything. Do you notice any patterns?

- As another experiment, sit down to a meal with the intention of devoting yourself to chewing. See how long you can chew on one bite of food until it disappears. Experiment with different amounts of chewing for each bite, and with different chewing speeds. Do you notice any difference between a well-chewed and an underchewed mouthful? Is there a difference in the taste or in the way it moves down your throat? Note your subjective experience of chewing. Do you enjoy it? Do you find yourself anxious or impatient? Is there a calming effect?

# 14

# *The Elements of Sweetness*

I t is certainly no secret that human beings like sweet things. The U.S. Department of Agriculture estimates that the average American consumes more than 125 pounds of sugar each year in the form of soft drinks, ice cream, chocolate, snacks, and other common foods. That's about thirty teaspoons of sugar each day for every person. Have you ever wondered what is behind the lure of sweetness? Is it the mere taste on our tongue and the rush of sugar in our blood that we long for? Or are there hidden reasons why sweet things play such a compelling role in our lives?

The desire for sweets is inborn and instinctual. Research reveals that as increasing amounts of sugar are added to a newborn's bottle, the rate of sucking increases. Small children offered a choice between a healthy food and a heavily sweetened one will overwhelmingly choose the sweet. Our first food, mother's milk, is naturally sweet, and some say it is very sweet when considering the highly sensitive taste buds

of an infant. From an evolutionary standpoint, our prefer-
ence for sweets is highly advantageous for survival. Not only
did it direct early hominids toward easily available ripe fruits
and vegetables, it kept them away from poisonous plants,
which are usually bitter in taste. No sweet foods are known
to exist in nature that are poisonous. But the longing for
sweets goes far beyond biology. It goes beyond the pleasure
of taste and beyond the instincts of the body.

In the spiritual tradition of India, it is said that if you could
taste the soul, it would be sweet. Indeed, the human condition in some of its most precious moments is perceived as
"sweet": "the sweet life," our "sweetheart," "sweet dreams,"
or "the sweet smell of success." Sweetness is an *experience*,
and food is just one doorway that leads us there.

The Sufis believe that every object and sensation on the
physical plane has a corresponding mirror image on higher
planes. In their view the sweetness of food (on the physical
level) is reflected in the sweetness of love (emotional), which
is reflected in the sweetness of divine ecstasy (spiritual). Even
though the sweetness of a chocolate truffle differs radically
from the sweetness shared between lovers, the metaphoric
connections still exist.

In fact, scientists have recently discovered a chemical com-
pound in chocolate—phenylethylamine—believed to mimic
the physiological sensations of love. Even more fascinating, in
the religious traditions of the Hindus, Taoists, and Tibetan
Buddhists, mystics have referred to ecstatic states where a
sensation of indescribable sweetness spontaneously arises in
the mouth. Contemporary accounts of this phenomenon are
widespread among meditators and practitioners of religious
traditions of the East and the West.

Furthermore, the Austrian philosopher-scientist Rudolf
Steiner pointed out the role various foods have played in the
evolution of consciousness in different historical epochs.

Sugar is seen as a food that has had a powerful effect in helping to expand personality force, creativity, and self-consciousness. Even today historians are at a loss to understand why so many wars have been fought over sugar and different spices. I offer this reason: Sugar and spices were the drugs of earlier cultures. When these foods were first introduced, their effect was even more powerfully narcotic and mind-expanding than they are today.

When we long for sweets, our desire is not just for food. Our longing is for the *experience of sweetness,* something we can taste on the tongue, in the heart, or in our most sacred thoughts. However, because it is more difficult to find a sweetheart or sweet Jesus, the mind often considers sweet foods an acceptable substitute. Food happens to be the most available form of the sweet experience. Can you see how we instinctively crave sweetness on several different levels? Do you understand why it is a perfectly natural biological phenomenon?

Sugary food is one of the most popular forms of substitute love. Its effect is even more potent when combined with the love-inducing chemicals in chocolate. The downside of repeated substitution is the same for sugar as it is for drugs, alcohol, or cigarettes: dependency. We become mechanically bound to sugar because it fulfills an immediate need and exerts a powerful narcotic effect.

It is important to note that the need for the sweet experience is inborn, but as every nutritional scientist knows, there is no physiological requirement for *refined* sugar in the diet. Quite the contrary. Excess sugar in the diet promotes tooth decay and obesity and has been implicated in heart disease, diabetes, hypoglycemia, immune deficiency diseases, digestive disorders, and allergies. Perhaps the most fascinating and best kept medical secret about sugar is that excessive consumption causes calcium loss, which leads to a much publicized disease of our day—osteoporosis.

Early research in this area revealed that despite normal levels of calcium in the blood, many people still experienced bone loss and periodontal decay. This led scientists to discover how minerals work in intricate balance. Precise ratios must be maintained by the body's homeostatic mechanism to ensure health. Both calcium and phosphorus work in optimal relationship when their ratio in the blood is 10:4. So even if our calcium level is normal or high, we may still have poor calcium absorption if phosphorus levels are off. Sugar has the physiological effect of lowering calcium levels and raising phosphorus. Even two teaspoons of sugar is enough to alter the sensitive 10:4 ratio. Coupled with heavy use of caffeine, the effects are even worse. Just three cups of coffee (without sugar) is enough to cause the excretion of 45 milligrams of calcium.

And if you think artificial sweeteners are the answer to your sugar cravings, consider this: In an American Cancer Society study of 78,000 women, those who consumed artificially sweetened foods gained *more* weight over a one-year period than those who consumed sugar-sweetened products. In another study students were *hungrier* after drinking artificially sweetened liquids than sugared ones. If sugar is a substitute for "the sweet experience," then artificial sweeteners are a substitute for a substitute. It's like using counterfeit money to buy fake diamonds.

Rather than using this information about sugar to label it as something bad, use the facts as a helpful tool for determining your dietary choices. Most of sugar's harmful effects are caused by excessive and habitual consumption. Moderate use of sugar is probably less harmful to the body than the stress created by resisting it or the guilt and self-rejection we feel from eating it.

More guilt and conflicts arise through eating sweets than any other food, and the reason is simple: Once we label the desire for sweets as bad (sinfully good, devilishly rich), we automatically fear it and fight it. We attempt to deny an inborn urge that *cannot* be suppressed. Imagine what would happen if scientists concluded that smiling was fattening and unhealthy. People would fight the urge to smile and feel guilty when a smile forced its way out. Some clever manufacturer would invent artificial smiles, a mask with a smile painted on it that people could wear to fulfill the natural inclination to smile but without the harmful effects. Consider sweets in the same light. The yearning for sweetness is simply the heart's desire to smile. And no amount of denial or artificial substitutes can change that.

From a physiological standpoint an urge for sweets arises for a number of different reasons. First, if we eat a large amount of refined sugar the body naturally craves more. This is because refined sugar has been stripped of the nutrients that occur in its natural state. Normally these vitamins and minerals assist in the metabolism of sugar in the body, but when refined sugar is eaten, the body must provide these nutrients from its own stores. This is one reason why excessive sugar consumption causes calcium loss through bones and teeth. The body pulls this nutrient from the most available source to help neutralize blood acidity and aid in sugar metabolism.

The end result is that the body goes into a "nutrient debt" and craves more food. Unfortunately it craves the same sugar that depleted it in the first place. To help you understand how the body can crave the very substance that is harming it, think of this analogy: When passing the scene of a car accident, most people are horrified yet traffic slows down to a near halt so motorists can take a long look. We fixate upon the image disturbing us. Likewise with a craving. We apply our brakes and fixate on the substance disturbing our system.

Another reason we crave sweets is because of high consumption of meat or salty foods. Simply put, the more meat and salt in the diet, the more sugar we desire. The reason for this is that from an energetic perspective, meat and salt are highly contractive foods (yang), and sugar is a highly expansive substance (ying). The more we consume of one, the more we crave the other to create balance. Many people with sugar dependencies report that their need for sugar drops significantly when they cut down on meat.

Interestingly enough, we crave sugar also when there is not enough protein in the diet. The reason for this is that opposites, in their extremes, change into one another. Extreme pleasure becomes painful. Extreme light is blinding (darkness). And lack of protein or meat, an extremely expansive condition, will cause us to crave the food we need least, an extremely expansive food like sugar. It is not unusual for people who switch to a vegetarian diet and have a lower protein intake to begin craving sweet foods. And vegetarians who eat too much refined sugar often have strong cravings for meat and fish.

Experiment with your diet to gain a better understanding of your urge for sweets. If it seems that you lack protein, increase your protein intake and observe what happens. If you consume a large amount of protein—especially in the form of meat, decrease the amount and notice how it affects your sugar urge. If you consume a good deal of refined sugar, try substituting other sweeteners such as rice syrup, barley malt, maple syrup, raw honey or sucanat (a natural unrefined sugar) and see if any positive changes occur.

Most importantly, remember that the yearning for the sweet experience is built into the human condition, and that by accepting this urge as a natural part of the eating process, we enable ourselves to enjoy the magical sensations that sweet foods inspire. Of equal importance is our respect for the powerful influence sweet substances can exert on the human body. In doing so we can learn to fulfill our desires without sacrificing our health. It may also help to remember that often, in yearning for sweet foods, we secretly yearn for something more. This something more may seem to be an elusive mystery. And that's what makes it so sweet.

## KEY LESSONS

- The desire for sweet foods is inborn and natural.

- Sweetness is an experience. It is sensed not only on the tongue but also in the heart and soul.

- Sweet foods are a powerful source of substitute love.

- By regulating and balancing different foods in the diet, we can successfully manage our urge for sweets.

## REFLECTIONS

- Do you desire sweet foods? When do you desire them most? Is there a correlation between your emotional state and the intensity of your need for something sweet?

- Do you fight and resist your urge for sweets? If so, do you consider sugary foods bad? Do you fear gaining weight? How can you change your attitude to sweets so that you can see them as neutral?

- Eat something sweetened with sugar and carefully note any physical symptoms or emotional changes in the next several hours. Are these changes beneficial?

- Completely eliminate sugar from your diet for one week. Note any difficulties that arise, any bodily changes, and any emotional responses.

- Compare the experience of sweetness between Coke and Diet Coke, a fruit drink sweetened with corn syrup and one made from 100 percent fruit juices, an organically grown grapefruit and an inorganic one. Note the nuances of sweetness and taste, your level of satisfaction, and any sensations in the body.

- Aside from food, what other experiences in your life would you categorize as sweet?

# 15

## Ordered Eating

Up till now we have discussed many aspects of "disordered eating." The question that naturally arises is what is "ordered eating"? What is a harmonious approach to eating, if indeed there is such a thing? We have already seen that the solutions of those who claim to have the answers to enlightened eating differ greatly from each other, and the key is to understand that all the perspectives on eating are, within certain limits, "correct." Each approach is composed of a small portion of a larger spectrum of nutrition, a piece of the bigger nourishment puzzle.

Through observation and study of the different nutritional approaches, I have synthesized what I consider to be the most important principles of each. I call this approach ordered eating. It is a collection of twenty of the best guidelines for eating and is useful as a reference tool, a way to compare our current perspective on eating to one much broader in scope.

Because I have chosen to make these guidelines as free of

nutritional dogma as possible, I have left out specifics about the best foods to eat, best combinations, and so on. As a result, the principles can be applied to almost any nutritional approach.

## THE PRINCIPLES OF ORDERED EATING

Ordered eating is:

1. *Intentional*     We eat because we choose to eat, not because we are compelled to do so through habit.

2. *Conscious*     We eat with awareness of the body, taking notice of atmosphere, company, taste, texture, posture, chewing, aroma, and all the sensations of the eating experience.

3. *Reflective*     We actively listen for the body's feedback: Did the food help or hinder the body, and what can we do next time to ensure a more fulfilling meal?

4. *Exploratory*     We understand eating to be a learning and exploration process, an ongoing journey through the unknown where both diet and body are continuously changing.

5. *Transformational*     Because our relationship to food mirrors our relationship to life, we work

with habits and attitudes about eating
to help transform ourselves at deeper
levels.

| | |
|---|---|
| 6. *Nourishing* | We understand that food nourishes by virtue of the following: |
| Type | Different foods either help or hinder biological function. |
| Quality | Foods of similar type vary in quality depending upon nutrient content; toxic residue level; and method of growing, storage, and preservation. |
| Preparation | The skill and awareness with which a food is cooked and prepared determines its effect. |
| Amount | The quantity of food eaten will determine its effect. |
| Timing | The timing of a meal determines its effect. Certain foods eaten at certain times of the day are more readily digested, while the amount of time between meals also affects digestive capacity. |
| 7. *Body-based* | We eat according to our body constitution and biochemical individuality. |
| 8. *Strategic* | We understand that diet functions on either maintenance, therapeutic, or experimental levels. |

| | |
|---|---|
| 9. *Personalized* | We understand that our food choices are regulated by our life-style. |
| 10. *Seasonal* | We include seasonal foods in our diet to benefit from biocosmic cycles. |
| 11. *Localized* | We include locally produced foods in our diet to benefit from bioregional cycles. |
| 12. *Synergistic* | We understand diet to work in synergy with other factors such as exercise, sleep cycles, breath patterns, and emotions. |
| 13. *Communal* | We understand that sharing a meal with others can be nourishing to them and to ourselves. |
| 14. *Intimate* | We understand that eating may be a personal experience of self. |
| 15. *Connected* | We are aware that eating connects us to the earth, soil, animals, plants, and waters, and that by nourishing them with thoughtful and conscientious methods, we nourish ourselves. |
| 16. *Mindful* | We understand the wisdom of balance and moderation in what we eat and what we believe about diet. |
| 17. *Spontaneous* | We understand that occasional episodes of imbalance, lack of moderation, and strategic rule-breaking are likely to occur and can be useful and instructive. |

| | |
|---|---|
| 18. *Broad-minded* | We understand that foods are neither morally good nor bad, and recognize the uselessness of judging anyone (including ourselves) for what they eat. |
| 19. *Liberating* | We understand that once a meal is finished, we need not continue to think or fantasize about food. |
| 20. *Joyous* | Above all else, we smile when we eat. |

Over the years I have utilized these principles as *guidelines* to uncover something that is already within me, instead of hard and fast rules that drive me to become what I am not yet ready to be. For example, I consistently eat seasonal foods, but I do not force myself to do so. I tried eating seasonal foods, it worked, and it became a natural and spontaneous aspect of my diet. I also eat many healthy, high-quality foods, but not because I think I should. They taste good, I enjoy them, and when I eat them my body in its own unique way says *yes*.

I should note that when I first started eating healthy foods, I did so as an experiment. I read about many nutritional principles and decided to test the effects of a healthy diet. Eating foods that were supposedly good for me was a new concept and did not come naturally. I recall the first time I ate seaweed. I was in a vegetarian restaurant in Boston and saw a special on the menu that had *nori* in it. The other ingredients in the dish sounded edible, so I ordered it because I had heard many wonderful things about the miraculous properties of seaweed. The experience of eating it did not seem miraculous at all. For days afterward a fishy odor lingered in my nose.

About a year later, having improved my level of health and

energy through experimenting with diet and exercise, I tried seaweed again. I could not believe how good it tasted and how great it felt. More than cultivating a taste for seaweed, I had cultivated a taste for health-enhancing foods.

The ordered eating guidelines are especially helpful because they focus not only on health but on attitude to health. For years I ate with tension and judged the eating habits of myself and others. After endless searching for the perfect diet, I reached a place inside myself that acknowledged that wherever I was as an eater, was okay. If I ate turkey or tuna, it was fine. If I wanted ice cream, I was okay. Even if I ate nachos and guacamole until I was sick, I was still okay. By breaking free of rules fueled by fear and judgment, I was able to make awakened choices that worked.

And, paradoxically, letting go of rules allowed me to return to them with renewed insight and a healthier momentum. I now have a lively appreciation for nourishment rather than a list of do's and don't's. This is one of the great pleasures I experience with diet—eating foods that I know are good for me and that also taste and feel good.

I still have quirks and problematic areas with eating; however, I do not create any tension or judgments about these parts of myself. I simply observe and experiment with great fascination. If I eat because I am upset, I do not create further tension by judging myself for eating out of an emotional need. I merely catalog this piece of information somewhere inside and stay alert to the benefits and drawbacks.

Once we accept the unpredictable nature of our bodies, our relationship to food becomes naturally exciting. It intrigues me to watch my food preferences change, how one week I will desire almond butter and then for months lose my taste for it, or how I'll crave raisin bran cereal in the morning for a period of time and then switch to oatmeal instead. For many people such shifts in food preferences are discomforting. And yet these changes are the essence of the eating experience.

It is quite rare to find someone who has created a successful working relationship to diet. Over the years I have observed only a handful of individuals who possess the qualities I seek most—a sense of aliveness, a radiant energy, a body that exudes health no matter what the age, and a personal philosophy that, for them, genuinely works. Despite the very different diets and life paths they follow, the "expert eaters" all have the following attributes in common:

- They eat with freedom from fear, worry, or guilt.

- They eat with both an intuitive understanding and knowledge of the body's changing nutritional needs.

- They accept their body as it is.

- They use diet as a transformational tool.

- They eat with joy.

Body size and food selection are not primary criteria for masterful eaters. As we have seen, one could have an ideal body or achieve a dream body weight yet still be unhappy, or we can eat what we consider the perfect foods yet still experience guilt, cravings, and ill health. The expert eaters, as do others, still encounter challenges with food. What distinguishes their mastery is attitude.

To some degree we are all disordered eaters. Each of us experiences some form of discord in our relationship to food simply because that is the nature of the game. None of us can escape imperfection in eating or in anything in life. So it is fruitless to attach any kind of stigma to our relationship to food.

Each of us, in our own way and our own time, is searching

for a nourishment that reflects who we are and how we wish to experience life. Some search for a fulfilling nutrition simply by eating what tastes good, some choose highly regimented diets, some abuse the body and learn the hard way, while others seem to eat what they want without any ill effects.

The bottom line is this: No diet is right or wrong. Any method of eating can provide a deeper nourishment as long as the missing ingredient—consciousness—is present. The ability to reflect on our relationship to food and the awareness that we can expand our perspective on eating at any moment help create the life we want most.

## KEY LESSONS

- Nutritional advice is most successful when it is used as a guideline to encourage rather than as a rule to enforce.

- We have created a good working relationship with diet when we face the usual problematic areas without adding further tension or self-judgment.

- With the right attitude many different dietary approaches can be practiced with equal success.

## REFLECTIONS

- Do you notice any guidelines of ordered eating that are already mainstays in your life? Which ones are they and how do you practice them? Do any of the guidelines stand out by virtue of their relative absence in your life? If you incorporated these missing principles, would your relationship to food be more balanced or fulfilling?

- Make a list of guidelines for your own system of ordered eating. Include as much specific information as you like, particularly about what to eat and what not to eat. See if you can create a realistic system and follow it for two weeks.

- Choose someone you live with or are close to and eat this person's exact diet for one day. Observe your reactions.

- What is your definition of an eating disorder?

- Think of someone you know whom you wish to model yourself on in terms of how they eat. List as many of their characteristics as you can. What benefits would you expect to receive if you ate as this person does?

- Think of someone you know who is a significant role model for you, regardless of eating habits. Does this person eat foods you consider bad? If so, what does this imply?

- As an experiment, pretend for one week that you love to wash dishes. Wash your dishes with enthusiasm and attention. Note any changes in your relationship to food.

- Invite someone for dinner whose company you really enjoy. Note your experience of the food. Invite someone whom you disapprove of on another evening. Note any changes in the eating experience.

- If you are having difficulties or challenges in your relationship to eating, be thankful to your food before each meal for a week. If you are not experiencing any difficulties, be thankful to your food for two weeks.

# 16

# *True Nourishment*

The questions I always return to when addressing any issue with food or nutrition is, What nourishes? What is it that truly feeds us and provides the satisfaction we seek? We believe that good nutrition nourishes us, and it does, yet it is easy to lose sight of all that nourishes and focus on nutrition alone. There is a wonderful scene in Woody Allen's movie *Sleeper* where he wakes up after two centuries of suspended animation. The scientists who have brought him out of this long sleep explain his plight, and one of the first questions he asks is, "Where are all my friends?" He is told that his friends are dead, to which he replies with his classic forlorn and quizzical look, "I don't understand it; they all ate organic rice."

The question of what nourishes is often difficult to answer because our dietary notions change constantly. What we thought was good to eat yesterday is not always what we think is good today. Since colonial times people have believed that red meat was the king of foods. It made you strong and healthy and was even better for you than the most commonly consumed and well-loved staple—pork. Since the late 1960s this trend has completely reversed. Red meat and pork are no longer considered staples, but foods to eat occasionally. In fact, most other foods once considered the center of a healthy diet—whole milk, eggs, butter, cheese, and potatoes—are now under attack in some scientific circles, while foods such as oat bran, which previously fed our farm animals, are now seen as the edibles of choice. As one senior citizen remarked, "First I learned to eat lots of meat and eggs because they made you healthy, then I learned you shouldn't eat them because they made you sick, but you should eat fish instead; then I learned you shouldn't eat fish because of toxic metals in fish fat, and now I'm told to take a fish liver oil supplement—fish fat—because it lowers your cholesterol."

Most nutritional assertions that originate from authoritative sources have a brief shelf life. Our nutritional information is not based on what is ultimately good to eat, but what we *believe* is good to eat at the time. Within this unstable state of affairs, one thing does remain constant—the connection between our relationship to food and our inner world. How we eat is a reflection of how we live. Our hurrying through life is reflected in hurrying through meals. Our fear of emotional emptiness is seen in our overeating. Our need for certainty and control is mirrored in strict dietary rules. Our looking for love in all the wrong places is symbolized in our use of food as a substitute for love.

The more we are aware of these connections, the greater the potential for our personal unfolding and inner satisfaction. For in changing the way we eat, we change the way we live. By focusing attention while eating, we learn to focus attention in any situation. By enjoying food, we begin to enjoy nourishment in all its forms. By loosening dietary restrictions, we learn to open up to life. By accepting our body as it is, we learn to love ourselves for who we are. And by eating with dignity, we learn to live with dignity.

Imagine for a moment all the different diets you have ever followed—the foods you ate as a newborn, a small child, a youth, a young adult, and on through the rest of your life. Who were these eaters? Where did they come from? Where did they go? What precipitates the change from one diet to the next? What will you be eating a year from now? Ten years from now?

I recall with a sense of awe my father lying in a hospital bed with tubes entering his nose, his mouth, and the veins in his arms, providing him with his only source of nourishment. Here was a human being, who fifty-eight years earlier had been born in a hospital with a feeding tube running from his mother to his belly, and now he was once more lying helplessly in a hospital. For all the diets he had ever followed, for all the bottles of vitamins, bagels and cream cheese with butter, and macrobiotic meals he had ever eaten, he was now, in some strange unearthly way, back where he had started.

What nourished him in his lifetime? What foods were good for him? Did he absorb the nutrients he needed? Did he accumulate too many toxins? Would the right diet have saved him? Perhaps he ate too much meat. Too much cholesterol. Too much salt. Not enough calcium. Not enough fiber . . .

When the body no longer flourishes, a new reality is seen, one that urges us forward into the unknown and backward to look upon what has been, to ask the question that may never have passed our lips, What nourishes?

We now understand that nourishment is not only nutrition. It is the *experience* of that nutrition—the *heart*iness, the sentiments, and the soul intention on which our eating is based. What nourishes is our relationship to food, our participation in the ongoing exploration of eating, the wonder, the joy, the confusion, the change, the uncertainty, the pain, the aliveness, the theories, the disputes, the shopping, the cooking, the sharing, the ripe watermelon, the over-cooked spaghetti, the healthy foods, the forbidden sweets, and the knowing that when a meal is finished, we will return for another and another and another.

Whether it is the eternal round of the seasons, the sun, the stars in the night sky, or the hunger in our body, we continually end up where we began, finding ourselves at similar crossroads and often with similar opportunities. At any moment we may begin life anew. Begin your relationship to food now. Rather than wait for a time that may never arrive to embrace all that nourishes, embrace it now.

Everyone eats, but how many of us have understood what it means to be an eater? Whether you know it or not, each time you eat you secretly make a commitment to continue to live.

And though we make this life-affirming choice whenever we eat, it often arises from a heart that is fearful, uncertain, and at times turned against itself. We fear our natural cravings and desires, search for perfection in health or body weight when it can never be found, and live in fear of failing at the impossible standards we set. We surround the eating process with *our* rules rather than accepting it as it is.

Agreeing to be an eater means a conscious, deliberate, ritualistic, and hopefully liberating choice. Birth itself was our original agreement to be an eater. It seems reasonable to believe that sometime early in our career, we agreed to be here, to wear diapers, learn finger painting, take spelling tests, have a sex drive, find a good-paying job, and ultimately to exit this world on the same round-trip ticket we arrived with. And in doing so, we agreed to the necessity of being an eater.

It is time to renew the agreement, to reacquaint ourselves with its terms, and to integrate it into our lifetime of eating experience. If we choose to live, we must choose to eat, and if we choose to eat, why not accept the reality of all that it means to be an eater if happiness and peace of mind are our ultimate goals? Here is a restatement of the original promise that we made long ago.

## THE EATER'S AGREEMENT

I hereby agree, from this day forward, to fully participate in life on earth. I agree to inhabit the appropriate vehicle for such participation—a body. As a requisite for the sustaining of that body, and of the life that dwells therein, I agree to be an eater. This agreement fully binds me for the duration of my stay on earth.

As an eater, I agree to hunger. I agree to have a body that needs food. I agree to eat food. I recognize that as the biological need to eat is fulfilled with greater awareness and efficiency, the benefits of my well-being will increase. I further acknowledge that ignorance of the eating process may cause undesirable consequences.

Because the essence of my participation in life is one of learning and exploration, I agree to experience uncertainty as an eater. I recognize there are a great variety of foods to choose from, and I may not know which to eat. I may have a choice of different nutritional approaches, and not know which to follow. I may have an assortment of habits, and not know how to manage them. I recognize that my relationship to food is a learning process, and I will inevitably make mistakes. Therefore, as an eater, I agree to accept my humanness and learn as I go along.

I acknowledge that as the body changes from infancy to old age, so will the eating process change. I recognize that my body may call for different foods as the days, seasons, and years progress. My dietary needs will also shift in accord with changes in my life-style and environment. I understand that there is no one perfect diet.

As an eater, I accept pain. I recognize that I may suffer pain when the body is disturbed by my choice of food or eating habits. I may also experience pain when emotional and spiritual hungers are confused with physical hunger. I further understand that eating to cure a pain that cannot be remedied by eating may bring even more pain.

I further agree to accept a body that is imperfect and vulnerable, that naturally decays with the passage of time. I recognize there will be moments when I am incapable of caring for it myself. I agree, then, that to live in a body is to need the help of others. I also agree to be vulnerable as an eater. I acknowledge that I will be helpless as an infant and will need to be fed. I may be equally helpless when I am old and unwell. I further recognize that even when I am fully capable, I may still need the warmth and care of someone who can feed me. Therefore, as an eater, I agree to be nourished by others.

If I have a woman's body, I acknowledge that I have a special relationship to eating and nourishment. I recognize that as a giver of life, I am the nourisher of life as well. Whether through my cooking or the milk of my body, I acknowledge that the union of food and love is a quality that marks my womanhood and has a profound effect on human-kind.

As an eater, I acknowledge the domain of the sacred. I recognize that the act of eating may be ritualized and inspired. It may be given symbolic meanings that are religious or spiritual in nature. It may even be joyous.

I further agree that eating is an activity that joins me with all humanity. I recognize that to be an eater is to be accountable for the care of the earth and its resources. I acknowledge that despite our differences, we are all ultimately nourished by the same source. As such, I agree to share.

I recognize that at its deepest level eating is an affirmation of life. Each time I eat I agree somewhere inside to continue life on earth. I acknowledge that this choice to eat is a fundamental act of love and nourishment, a true celebration of my existence. As a human being on earth, I agree to be an eater. I choose life again and again and again. . . .

# About the Author

Marc David has a master's degree in psychology and nutrition and has been a marketing, management, and technical consultant in the food-, vitamin-, and fitness-related industries. He has a great deal of energy and loves to go beyond his limits, particularly in mountain biking, trail running, and cross-country skiing. In addition to writing and private counseling, he lectures and teaches, especially at the Kripalu Center for Yoga and Health in the Berkshires.